# THE
# TRENT & MERSEY CANAL

# THE
# TRENT & MERSEY CANAL

*by*
*Jean Lindsay*

WITH PLATES AND MAPS

DAVID & CHARLES
NEWTON ABBOT LONDON NORTH POMFRET (VT)

**British Library Cataloguing in Publication Data**

Lindsay, Jean, b. 1926
    The Trent & Mersey Canal – (Canals of the British Isles).
    1. Trent and Mersey Canal, Eng. – History
    I. Title     II. Series
    386'.48'094246       HE436.Z5T/
    ISBN 0 7153 7781 7

Library of Congress Catalog Card Number: 79–51089

Typeset by Ronset Ltd., Darwen, Lancashire.
Printed in Great Britain
by Redwood Burn Ltd., Trowbridge
for David & Charles (Publishers) Limited
Brunel House   Newton Abbot   Devon

Published in the United States of America
by David & Charles Inc
North Pomfret   Vermont 05053 USA

FOR JOHN AND MOLLIE

# CONTENTS

*Page*

*List of Illustrations*     9

1 The Fight for the Canal     11

2 The Construction of the Trent & Mersey Canal     33

3 The Construction of the Branches     54

4 The Years of Success     74

5 Railway Competition     113

6 Commercial Decline     135

7 The Survival of the Trent & Mersey Canal     157

*Acknowledgements*     163

*Notes*     165

*Index*     173

# LIST OF ILLUSTRATIONS

PLATES

|  | Page |
|---|---|
| Preston Brook: the junction of the Trent & Mersey and Bridgewater Canals | 65 |
| Preston Brook: the south entrance to Preston Brook tunnel | 65 |
| The Anderton lift from the River Weaver | 66 |
| An aerial view of the Anderton lift | 66 |
| The Harecastle tunnel: the north end | 83 |
| The Harecastle tunnel: the south end | 83 |
| The Caldon branch at Hanley | 84 |
| The Hazelhurst locks on the Caldon branch | 84 |
| The Hazelhurst aqueduct | 101 |
| The Holly Bush Inn at Denford | 101 |
| Josiah Wedgwood's factory at Etruria | 102 |
| The Colwich lock | 102 |
| The Swan Inn at Fradley Junction | 119 |
| The weir at Alrewas | 119 |
| Wychnor Church | 120 |
| The Malt Shovel Inn at Shardlow | 120 |

MAPS AND PLANS

| 1 | The Trent & Mersey Canal and its connections | 21 |
| 2 | Preston Brook and Northwich | 34 |
| 3 | Middlewich and Kidsgrove | 50 |
| 4 | Stoke-on-Trent and Stone | 61 |
| 5 | The Caldon Canal | 79 |
| 6 | Great Haywood and Rugeley | 93 |
| 7 | Alrewas and Burton-on-Trent | 111 |
| 8 | Swarkestone and Shardlow | 126 |
| 9 | Anderton in 1872 | 136 |
| 10 | Plan for the Anderton lift | 139 |

# I

# The Fight for the Canal

THE Trent & Mersey, or Grand Trunk, was a pioneer concern
not only in its vision of cheap sea-to-sea transport from Hull to
Liverpool, but also in its concept of a trunk route linking with
other major inland waterways. It played a key role in the transport
and industrial revolutions of the late eighteenth and early nineteenth centuries, and its prosperity encouraged many other canal
promoters so that industry and agriculture were provided with
relatively cheap water carriage throughout the British Isles.

The main inspiration for the canal came from Francis Egerton,
third and last Duke of Bridgewater, who completed his Manchester to Worsley canal in 1761, thus considerably reducing the
price of coal from his mines at Worsley. His example provided an
incentive to the growing Staffordshire pottery industry, whose
manufacturers hoped that their pots, clay and flint could be
transported safely and cheaply by the same means. In this desire,
not entirely fulfilled because of varying degrees of monopolistic
control, they were joined by salt producers in Cheshire, brewers
in Burton-on-Trent, iron and coal merchants in Staffordshire
and cheesemongers in Derbyshire, Staffordshire and Cheshire.

The canal's promotion campaign lasted at least fifteen months,
and during that time many plans were drawn up, often backed by
surveys, petitions and pamphlets.[1] By the end of the eighteenth
century the Trent & Mersey was already a commercial success,
and Staffordshire had become a network of canals, forming the
centre of the canal cross joining the Trent, the Mersey, the
Severn and the Thames.

The history of the canal, however, began with a campaign of
publicity and private intrigue in the remote moorland area of
Staffordshire. Its promotion involved a battle between the
Trustees of the Weaver Navigation, who wished the canal to

terminate at its western end in the Weaver at Northwich, and the
Duke of Bridgewater, who wanted the canal's western terminus
to be a junction with his canal at Preston Brook. The Weaver
trustees promoted rival schemes to try to gain acceptance of their
plan; the Duke's aim was not made clear until about two months
before the canal was authorised. Other industrialists, led by Josiah
Wedgwood of Burslem and encouraged by Erasmus Darwin,
promoted the canal politically and finally accepted the Duke of
Bridgewater's scheme.

The 'Burslemites' were mostly concerned with the pottery
industry around Burslem. Agriculture was the main occupation
of the area, but its isolation had been lessened by the construction
of turnpike roads.[2] Josiah Wedgwood (1730–95) was the out-
standing leader in the movement for the advancement of civilisa-
tion in Staffordshire. His ideas on transport and the pottery
industry were largely responsible for the development of the
Potteries which, by their products, enhanced England's reputation abroad and created a unique region.

The modern city of Stoke-on-Trent developed from the ancient
parishes of Stoke-upon-Trent and Wolstanton, with the two
manors of Tunstall and Newcastle controlling most of the area
of the present city. Tunstall included Burslem, and Newcastle
comprised Penkhull and Boothen, Hanley and Shelton, Clayton
and Seabridge, Botteslow, Longton, and part of Fenton. By the
Reform Act of 1832 Stoke became a parliamentary borough,
represented by two MPs; it included the townships of Penkhull
with Boothen, Tunstall, Burslem, Hanley, Shelton, Fenton Vivian,
Lane End, Fenton Culvert and Longton, the Vill of Rushton
Grange and the hamlet of Sneyd. Hanley with Shelton became
a borough in 1857; Penkhull and Boothen were taken into the
borough of Stoke-on-Trent in 1874; Longton and Lane End
became the borough of Longton in 1865; Burslem became a
borough in 1878; Tunstall and Fenton became urban districts in
1894; and on 31 March 1910 the six towns of Burslem, Tunstall,
Hanley, Stoke, Fenton and Longton became the county borough
of Stoke-on-Trent. This amalgamation, with the addition of
Newcastle-under-Lyme, made up the region of the Potteries.[3]

The chief reason why this region became so important for the
manufacture of pottery was not the availability of raw materials
but the fortuitous combination of Josiah Wedgwood's skill in

promoting the Trent & Mersey Canal with his ability to develop high-quality porcelain. Other entrepreneurs such as Minton, Adams, and Spode (who was the first English manufacturer to use bone in the preparation of white china) also contributed to the industry's success. The Staffordshire industry in the sixteenth and seventeenth centuries had been based on the red-burning clays of the area (which were not especially remarkable), and on the availability of galena (lead-sulphide) for glazing and coal for firing the clay. As timber became scarcer coal grew in importance, but the necessary combination of raw materials was not peculiar to north Staffordshire. In the late seventeenth and the eighteenth centuries the south Yorkshire coalfield had a similar-sized pottery industry, but in the absence of an entrepreneur like Wedgwood the manufacture did not develop; in fact it declined, largely because of competition from Staffordshire. The dairy industry of Staffordshire and Cheshire provided a local centre for butter and cheese, and Uttoxeter in particular was a very important market for butter-pots. This provided an incentive to earthenware production and between 1710 and 1715 there were forty-seven potworks in Burslem and Hanley.[4]

The Saxon potters from Delft, David and John Elers, (who were once silversmiths), are believed to have come from Holland with William III in 1688; they established a potwork at Bradwell near Burslem in 1693. They are said to have introduced salt glaze, although an examination of one of their kilns seems to prove that it was unsuitable for this process.[5] Salt glazing became popular in the early eighteenth century, and in 1720 John Astbury developed a salt-glazed ware that was all white. This involved bringing white clay from Devon and Cornwall, to which calcined flint was added. These materials could be brought up the River Weaver or the River Trent.

In 1759 Wedgwood rented the Ivy House Works in Burslem at £10 per annum, and in 1762 he transferred the firm to the Brick House Works. Queen Charlotte accepted a set of Wedgwood's cream ware in 1765; thereafter it became known as 'Queen's ware' and Wedgwood was appointed royal potter.[6] The coarse ware of the Potteries was transformed into stoneware of refinement, and Wedgwood, by employing artists like John Flaxman, who designed white decoration as relief on a coloured background, and through his own classical tastes, raised the reputation of the Potteries, so that when cheap transport was available, Staffordshire wares attained world-wide fame.

The engineer of the Trent & Mersey Canal was James Brindley (1716–72), who was born into a poor family in Tunsted in the parish of Wormhill in Derbyshire. He was a millwright by trade, and before turning to canal engineering he built, among other things, flint-mills in Staffordshire. He was largely self-educated. While he was apprenticed to the wheelwright Abraham Bennett, near Macclesfield, from 1733 to 1742, he taught himself to write, but the art of spelling eluded him: as Paul Mantoux observed, he could never spell the word 'navigation'.[7] Arnold Bennett, who was born in 1867 in Stoke-on-Trent, claimed in an article in the *Daily Express* on 6 February 1928 that his family was descended from an illegitimate offspring of James Brindley. He does not seem to have substantiated the claim, but Brindley did have a natural son by Mary Bennett of Burslem. Mary Bennett was not related to Abraham, and the child was baptised John Bennett on 31 August 1760.[8]

After his apprenticeship, James Brindley began work as a wheelwright at Leek; from his note-books, of which several have survived, the varied nature of his work can be seen. He is sometimes compared with Richard Arkwright, for both men seemed to arouse envy and disbelief in their talents. Arkwright, however, was a superb businessman and made a fortune, while Brindley never lived the life of a wealthy man. In March 1760, with his partners John Brindley, Hugh Henshall, John Gilbert and Thomas Gilbert, he purchased Turnhurst estate; this included Golden Hill Colliery, into which branch canals were later made out of the Harecastle tunnel, so that coal could be loaded directly into the boats. The part-share in the estate shows that Brindley was not impoverished, even at that date. Samuel Smiles certainly exaggerated Brindley's low rates of pay.[9]

Brindley's first patron was Granville, second Earl Gower of Trentham (1721–1803), who was created Marquess of Stafford in 1786. He was the brother-in-law and friend of the Duke of Bridgewater, and the pottery village of Burslem was situated between Leek and his estate at Trentham. The brothers John and Thomas Wedgwood worked as potters at Burslem, and they employed Brindley to build flint-mills in order to increase the supply of flint powder. In 1750 Brindley built a windmill near Burslem for John Wedgwood, and he developed an improved mill for grinding flints. Brindley's fame, however, was to rest on his canal works, and around 1758 he was engaged on a survey for a 40-mile canal from Stoke-on-Trent to Wilden Ferry, which had been commissioned by Thomas Broade, Lord Anson and Earl Gower. Brindley was probably referring to this survey when he wrote on 5 February 'novocion 5 days' and on 19 February 'about the novogation 3 days'.[10] The *Derby Mercury* of 7 December 1758 described the scheme for a 'Cut to be 8 yards wide and 1 yard deep with Locks to pound the water and make it dead as the Canals in Holland.' The report went on to give the estimated traffic per annum with the estimated rate of tonnage:

| | | |
|---|---|---|
| Pots, clay, flint, etc | 6,000 tons at 5s per ton | £1,500 |
| Cheese | 1,000 tons | £250 |
| Corn, salt, malt | 1,000 tons | £250 |
| Ironmongery and trade goods | | £250 |
| Building material | at 2s 6d per ton | £125 |
| Pig iron | 1,000 tons at 5s per ton | £250 |
| Coal | 20,000 at 1s 6d per ton | £1,500 |
| | | £4,125 |

Plus a further 50 per cent for shorter-distance traffic.

Hugh Henshall, a land surveyor and part-owner of Turnhurst estate, drew a map of this proposed canal from the Trent at Wilden Ferry to Longbridge. This map showed three branches: one to Newcastle-under-Lyme, one to King's Bromley Common near Lichfield, and one to near Tamworth. It was entitled 'A Plan for a Navigation chiefly by Canal from Longbridge near Burslem in the County of Stafford to Newcastle, Lichfield and Tamworth and to Wilden in the County of Derby. By James Brindley. Revised and approved by John Smeaton 1760.' Henshall acted as Brindley's cartographer, and later, when the branches had been dropped and the communication with the Duke of Bridgewater's canal had been planned and accepted, he drew a revised map of the intended canal.[11]

In 1761 John Smeaton wrote his report on the practicability of a navigable canal 'from Wilden ferry, in the county of Derby, to King's Bromley Common, near Litchfield; and from thence in several branches, the first leading to Longbridge, near Burslem, the second to Newcastle under Lime, the third to the city of Litchfield; and the fourth to the river Tame, at or near Fazeley bridge, near Tamworth, all in the county of Stafford, as projected by Mr. James Brindley, Engineer'. In November 1760 Smeaton had 'carefully viewed and considered the tracts of ground' through which the proposed canal and its branches were to pass, and he had compared his survey with 'the plans and levels produced by Messrs. Brindley and Henshall'. Smeaton surveyed the rivers Trent and Tame, and he concluded that sufficient water could be collected from the streams to supply the canal and its branches. He noted that in many places the Trent was winding, shallow and subject to flooding, and he concluded that a separate canal would be preferable to one making use of the river. In particular, Smeaton considered that the navigable part of the Trent from Burton to Wilden Ferry was so much obstructed by shoals and currents that a canal would be more practicable.

Smeaton praised Brindley's judicious use of level commons and waste grounds, and 'in general ... the most barren lands that could be found in any wise to agree with the course'. He considered that the branch of the canal to Longbridge could be extended 'so as to join the navigable river that falls into the west sea', presumably the Weaver; and he suggested avoiding a considerable part of the ascent by a deep cut through the summit at Harecastle. Smeaton stated that the extension could be supplied with water from springs on the adjacent hills, and that there would be an increasing supply of water from the coal-pit drains.

Smeaton suggested that the navigation between Wilden Ferry and Gainsborough should be improved, either by 'an extension of the main canal from Wilden Ferry to the tide's way' or by some other means. He agreed with Brindley that the canal should be 'about 8 yards at the water line.' His estimate for the total work was £100,198. The report shows that Smeaton approved of Brindley's original plan, and that he, and possibly Hugh Henshall, contributed to the final scheme; but his plan for a sea-to-sea canal was not adopted.[12]

The need for an extension of the canal to the sea at the western end was certainly recognised by the Staffordshire manufacturers, who had great difficulty in transporting goods to the coast and in bringing raw materials to the area. Overland transport by waggon, even on turnpike roads, was not entirely satisfactory for heavy or delicate goods. There was no navigable river: the Trent rises near Biddulph in north Staffordshire, but navigation was rendered impossible by shoals and meanders and by changes in the volume and depth of the water. As a result of an act passed in 1699, navigation from Wilden Ferry to Burton-on-Trent was possible; but an attempt in 1714 to secure further improvement proved unsuccessful. Throughout the seventeenth century, the Trent had been navigable as far as Nottingham. In 1717 Thomas Congreve produced a plan for a canal 70 miles long to join improved stretches of the rivers Penk and Stour. This was not adopted, but the Staffordshire & Worcestershire Canal, which received the royal assent on 14 May 1766, the same date as the Trent & Mersey, used a similar plan, and employed Brindley as its engineer. The Staffordshire & Worcestershire Canal ran from its junction with the Trent & Mersey at Great Haywood to enter the Severn at Stourport; it thus linked the Severn with the Trent.

The 'canal idea', as Hugh Malet calls it, can be said to have originated in England with the Bridgewater navigation from the Duke's coal-mines at Worsley to Castlefield (Manchester). The Duke's canal, planned and constructed by his land-agent, John Gilbert (1724–95), with assistance from James Brindley, was independent of a river-bed and was supplied with water from the soughs or adits of the Duke's coal-mines. The Exeter Canal had been built between 1564 and 1566; and the Sankey Brook (St Helens) Canal is often regarded as the first modern canal, as most of it was opened in 1757 and it was independent of a river-bed. The Duke earned his title of 'the father of inland navigation', however, because he showed that canals could be extremely profitable. He was inspired by the Grand Canal of Languedoc, which linked the Atlantic and the Mediterranean; he had noted the canal section between Agde and Toulouse, which was supplied by feeders, during his Grand Tour in 1754. The Duke's canal, unlike most other English canals, was financed entirely by loans and private resources, not by a company. The act limited the price of the Worsley coal in Manchester to 4d a cwt for forty years, which was half the average price of coal in Manchester; and the Duke maintained a price of $3\frac{1}{2}$d a cwt until 1793.[13] The Bridgewater navigation, however, was important not only as a supplier of cheap coal but also as a source of inspiration to other canal builders.

In 1795 John Aiken claimed that the Corporation of Liverpool had, in 1755, employed 'Mr. Taylor of Manchester and Mr. Eyes of Liverpool to take surveys with a view to determining the practicability of joining the river Trent with the Weaver or the Mersey'; and this claim has been repeated by numerous authors. Although Aiken says the surveyors declared the scheme to be practicable, there is no reference to the matter in the corporation's surviving minute-books.[14] It is mentioned, however, in one manuscript version of section II of a pamphlet which was written by Josiah Wedgwood's partner Thomas Bentley to promote the Trent & Mersey Canal. This manuscript, which survives in the Wedgwood Collection of Keele University Library, asserts that the scheme was 'first proved to be practicable by the survey of Messrs. Taylor of Manchester and Mr. Eyes of Liverpool, done in the year 1755 at the expense of the Liverpool merchants; and chiefly promoted by the late Mr. Hardman . . . one of the representatives of that borough'. John Hardman was one of the great Liverpool merchants and was elected MP for the town in 1754; he died on 1 December 1755.[15] It is probable that the earlier version was correct, and that it was the merchants and not the corporation who financed the survey.[16] In a letter to Erasmus Darwin in April 1765, Josiah Wedgwood referred to a survey which had been made by Mr Eyes of Liverpool in 1757, a year before Brindley's; but this survey is no longer extant.[17] On 3 July 1765 Liverpool Corporation recorded that, after a 'further representation' to the council by Josiah Wedgwood on the 'intended navigation from the Trent to the Mersey', they had decided to make up their previous order for 50 guineas to £200. On 11 December of the same year the council pledged its support for the bill, and asked that a letter recommending it should be sent to MPs in Lancashire and the adjacent counties.[18]

Brindley's survey of 1758 suggested the possibility of connections and branches to link the 'Cheshire Rivers and the River Severn and finally to connect the Counties through which the R. Trent flows with all parts of the Kingdom'.[19] In the same year Henry Bradford had proposed that the rivers Trent and Tame should be improved and made navigable as far as Tamworth.[20] A letter from Josiah Wedgwood to Erasmus Darwin in April

1765 mentioned Darwin's suggestion that the canal, which was at this stage envisaged as running from the Weaver to Wilden Ferry, should have one branch to Lichfield, Tamworth and Birmingham, and another from Stoke to Newcastle-under-Lyme. The cost of this proposal was estimated at £700 a mile, excluding the cost of the act. On 23 December 1765, however, Josiah Wedgwood wrote to Thomas Bentley: 'We have indeed given up the thoughts of encumbering our petition with any branches at all, but shall cross the Trent twice . . . in order to facilitate a junction with Lichfield, Birmingham &c'.[21] The act contained no provision for branches, and these therefore required further bills.

Early in 1765 Erasmus Darwin of Lichfield, who was a Fellow of the Royal Society and a man of some literary talent, had discussed with Josiah Wedgwood the idea of a canal joining the east and west coasts of England. Like Wedgwood, Darwin was a member of the Lunar Society of Birmingham, which had been established by Matthew Boulton. James Watt was also a regular member, and so was Joseph Priestley. Darwin was an enthusiastic supporter of Wedgwood, and as a man of letters he offered many suggestions about how to promote the canal.[22] Wedgwood himself was typical of those 'captains of industry' who were now challenging the power and status of the landed aristocracy. He was the son of Thomas Wedgwood, a Burslem potter; at the age of nine, when his father died, he was apprenticed to his brother Thomas. In 1742 he caught smallpox, and during his convalescence he studied books on Greek and Roman art which profoundly influenced his style of pottery. One leg was badly affected by smallpox and had to be amputated in 1768, but the illness made Wedgwood an enthusiast for the glories of ancient Greece, Etruria and Rome. The new factory which he built near Burslem in 1769 was called Etruria, and the pieces made on the opening day, 13 June, were engraved with the motto *Artes Etruriae renascuntur*, 'The arts of Etruria are reborn'.[23]

Thomas Bentley (1731–80) was born at Scropton in Derbyshire. He was an intelligent and cultured man who became, after 1769, a partner of Josiah Wedgwood. He was a contributor to the *Monthly Review* and the founder of the Warrington Academy. As Wedgwood's partner he was chiefly concerned with sales management, and he was responsible for the London shop in

Greek Street.[24] Like Wedgwood he was ruthless in his promotion of the Trent & Mersey Canal.

By 1765, after years of discussion, the plans for this canal had reached an advanced stage. The manufacturers were led by Josiah Wedgwood and Earl Gower. At this date the canal was to run from Wilden Ferry through the Potteries to join either the Weaver or the Mersey. The canal route favoured by the Weaver trustees was the one by which the canal would join the Weaver at Winsford or Northwich, so that there would be access to the Mersey. There were others who wanted the canal to join the Mersey directly at a location below Hempstones, or who suggested that it should join the Bridgewater Canal at Agden, which would give access to the river at Hempstones. The Duke of Bridgewater wanted it to join his canal, which was already proceeding from Longford Bridge to the Mersey at Hempstones. The royal assent for this canal had been obtained on 24 March 1762.[25]

It was essential that Wedgwood's faction should be united, so it was in some exultation that he wrote to Thomas Bentley, 'Merchant in Liverpool', on 2 January 1765, to tell him that he had defeated a plan put forward by Thomas Gilbert MP (1720–1798), the land-agent of Earl Gower and legal agent of the Duke of Bridgewater, and by Samuel Garbett, a rich industrialist in Birmingham, to have commissioners to control the canal instead of a company of proprietors. Wedgwood had appealed to Earl Gower's 'candour and humanity', and had thus won him over to his side.[26] Samuel Garbett continued to support the canal project until the end of 1765, when Wedgwood wrote to Bentley: 'We have now no great expectation of any assistance from Birmingham. Mr. Garbett gave me reason to expect a considerable subscription there, £300, he mentioned, towards obtaining the Act of Parliament but now it seems he does not like our plan of having it executed by Proprietors as they will be apt to make the profits as much as they can.' Garbett was to remain 'neuter', except that he wanted to prevent an unreasonable tonnage being placed upon goods between Wychnor and Wilden Ferry.[27]

Thomas Gilbert, the elder brother of John, was MP for Earl Gower's pocket borough of Newcastle-under-Lyme from 1763 to 1768. He later became MP for Lichfield, and was responsible for several changes in the English Poor Law. Earl Gower, with

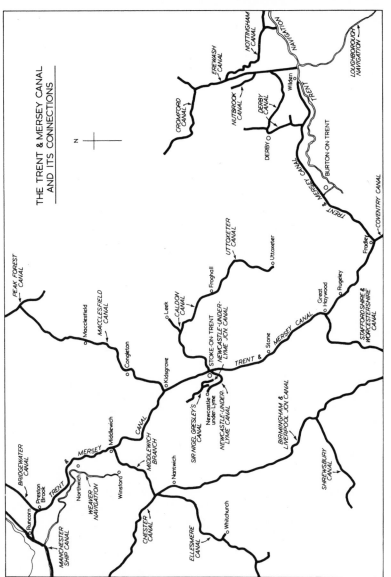

1 The Trent & Mersey Canal and its connections

his estate at Trentham, was an influential figure in Staffordshire, for which he was Lord Lieutenant. His political influence, and that of the Duke of Bridgewater, were crucial to the success of the canal. Samuel Garbett wrote to Wedgwood on 18 April 1765: 'I don't see any alarming opposition, for all arguments from common landholders are no more than General arguments against all inland Navigation, and will be laugh'd at unless supported by a few such as Lord Gower and the Duke of Bridgewater, who have great and ministerial weight.'[28] Earl Gower was a valued friend of Wedgwood, and was much interested in canals. In 1764 he had formed a company with the Gilbert brothers to promote the private Donnington Wood Canal, which ran through his estate.[29]

In order to persuade the promoters of the canal to form a junction with their river, the Weaver trustees not only planned a suitable route for the canal but also drew up favourable tonnage rates on the Weaver for goods passing to and from the canal. The trustees feared that the proposed canal, if it did not join the Weaver, would pose a real threat to their trade. The town of Northwich produced about 24,000 tons of salt annually, and was supplied via the Sankey and Weaver navigations with about 27,000 tons of coal. If coal could be supplied more cheaply from Staffordshire, this would enable the Cheshire salt-mines to compete with France and Spain for the Newfoundland fisheries trade. The Weaver was also dependent on the transport of white salt and rock salt, about 54,000 tons being shipped annually from Winsford to Northwich.[30] There were complaints about the maintenance of the Weaver, and after a conflict between the trustees and the Liverpool merchants an amending act was obtained in 1760. This act, 33 Geo II c 49, set up a new organisation of 105 trustees.[31] Throughout the eighteenth century, these trustees were drawn from the landed gentry of Cheshire; and the trust was a public one, the profits of which went towards subsidising the county's rates.[32]

In 1765 all groups of promoters intensified their efforts through personal contact, through pamphlets, and through the press. On 2 January 1765 Wedgwood wrote to Bentley: 'As the Canal will come very near Warrington on your plan, cannot you set something a going there, a subscription for going to Parliament will be most wanted and a separate Petition from that place would not be amiss.' He went on to mention manufacturers who would support the petition, and asked Bentley to print a thousand pamphlets in support of the navigation. Pamphlets played a large part in the campaign, and Bentley was to produce a masterly one himself.

On 6 March 1765 Josiah wrote to his brother John regarding a meeting with James Brindley on the subject of a canal from 'Hull or Wilden Ferry to Burslem agreeable to a Survey Plan before taken'. This presumably refers to Brindley's plan of 1758 for a cut from Wilden Ferry to Stoke; at that stage the question of the western terminus was not the vital issue which it later became. Josiah continued: 'Our Gent^m seem very warm in setting this matter on Foot again, and I could scarcely withstand the pressing invitations I had from all present, to undertake a journey or two for that purpose, we are to have another meeting at Hanley tomorrow and perhaps Wednesdays post shall know the result.'[33]

By 27 April 1765 Josiah Wedgwood was able to write to Bentley: 'We have begun to make the scheme public and intend with the assistance of our friends to continue a paper or two weekly in the *St James Chronicle* and to prevail with the Newsprinters of Liverpool, Manchester, Chester, Nottingham and Birmingham to insert them into their Papers. The subject is interesting and *will be* popular we therefore hope they will have no objection to employing a part of their paper for the article of Inland Navigation.' In this letter Wedgwood referred to Samuel Garbett's letter of 18 April, asking for Bentley's opinion of Garbett's plan to abuse the promoters as 'wild Schemers, and wonder at the impudence of upstart Mechanicks, and that they would imagine old families would permit their lands to be cut through for a nest of pilferers, to pass the Country by day and night &c'. Garbett's idea was that these foolish arguments would be answered by the promoters and 'be of use to prevent real opposition'.[34]

A meeting with John Gilbert had been held in April 1765, and on 15 April Josiah Wedgwood informed Erasmus Darwin that Gilbert, on being shown the plan of the canal, had 'immediately ask'd if it could not join the Dukes Canal which wo'd be allmost as near a way to Liverpool, and much nearer to Manchester and save our locking down into the River, for which we might afford

to give his Grace a small tonnage'.[35] In a subsequent letter to
Darwin, undated but presumably written in April, Josiah Wedgwood made reference to various pamphlets in the campaign,
including that of 'Mr Whitworths'. Wedgwood continued: 'I
do not know anything of the merits of the latter or its Author,
but assure you he bears no great Character among the Gentlemen
here, but rather a laughable one.'[36] Sir Richard Whitworth had
been at Eton and Cambridge, and his estate was at Batchacre
Grange in Staffordshire. He became MP for Stafford and was more
intelligent than Wedgwood's 'Gentlemen' appreciated, although
he impoverished himself by extensively improving his estate.[37] In
*A General History of Inland Navigation*, written by John Phillips
and published anonymously in 1785, Whitworth's plan was
described under the heading 'The Advantages of Inland Navigation'. Essentially, he proposed to link the ports of Liverpool,
Bristol and Hull by joining the rivers Weaver, Trent and
Severn.[38] Whitworth's ideas were supported by the Weaver
trustees, but his scheme did not link the Potteries to the Trent &
Mersey, and did not go near Birmingham.

The trustees were making every effort, at this stage, to win
over the Burslemites. At a general meeting on 5 December 1765
the trustees decided, despite their financial insecurity, to support
two rival schemes in a desperate bid to make the Burslemites join
the Weaver. One of the schemes was based on that of Sir Richard
Whitworth, and included a canal from Winsford via Checkley
Brook to Wrinehill. According to one of the trustees, George
Heron, this would avoid the Harecastle tunnel, and would mean
that goods could be carried from Checkley Brook to Liverpool
at a charge of 6s for freight and tonnage.[39] The other plan was
promoted chiefly by Charles Roe (1715–81), who had been a silk
merchant in Macclesfield but was now a copper merchant. In
1765–6 Roe supported a plan, which was ultimately a failure,
for a canal to link Macclesfield with Stockport and Manchester
and also with the Weaver Navigation. The bill stated that the
canal was to proceed from Witton Bridge via Nether Knutsford,
Macclesfield and Stockport to Manchester; the total length was to
be 37 miles. The Macclesfield plan was publicised in the *Manchester
Mercury*, which advertised meetings where the proposal was to be
discussed. These were held on 3, 12 and 26 December 1765, and
Charles Roe was appointed one of the collectors of subscriptions.

On 12 December 1765 Wedgwood wrote to Bentley informing him of the meeting of the 'Cheshire Gentlemen' which had taken place that day. He declared their scheme to be 'practicable', and said that if it was continued to Wilden Ferry, as he believed was intended, it would provide a navigable communication between Liverpool and Hull. Although Wedgwood had at first regarded the plan 'merely as a Bug Bear to us', he did not think it should be treated altogether as a 'chimerical scheme'. The intentions of the Duke were still far from clear to him. Early in July 1765, Wedgwood had written to his brother John about the Duke's interest in the Trent & Mersey Canal. He had spent eight hours with 'his Grace', who had given him an order for a complete table-service of cream ware. Later in the visit, along with John Sparrow (1737–1822), a lawyer from Newcastle-under-Lyme, he had had the pleasure of a 9-mile sail on the Duke's canal 'thro a most delightful vale to Manchester'.[40]

In his letter to Bentley on 12 December 1765, Wedgwood described the Duke as 'our patron' and praised his patriotism. He added, however:

> It grieved one to suspect such a character sho'd mean to serve himself only at the expense of what is most dear to a people by whom he is so much beloved. I hope his views are more liberal, more extended and more worthy a character so greatly respected, but it will be our truest policy as you advise that whatever be his *motives* we endeavour to make his actions contribute to the execution of our plan which is certainly calculated to serve the public more effectually than any other that hath yet been chalked out.

Wedgwood believed that the Duke of Bridgewater intended to bring a canal to Liverpool 'some way and some time – neither of which circumstances were determined'. This vagueness was still in evidence even in the act authorising the Trent & Mersey Canal, which said that the canal would join the River Mersey 'at or near a certain place called Runcorn Gap'. There seems little doubt, however, that the Duke had intended from the first to take over the carrying trade between Manchester and Liverpool from the Mersey & Irwell Co, and that he had considered the possibility of a link with a canal from the Trent to the Mersey long before 1766.[41]

Thomas Bentley was almost as active as Josiah Wedgwood himself in the promotion of the Trent & Mersey Canal. On 29 July 1765, Josiah wrote to his brother John that Mr Bentley was 'new framing' a pamphlet on inland navigation with 'a particular account of our design to unite the Trent and Weaver'. He also listed the influential people he was about to meet in connection with their 'scheme of navigation'. These included the Duke of Bridgewater, Lord Grey, Sir Walter Bagot and Sir William Wolseley; and Josiah expressed his hope that 'with a little very honest management' he could 'make this turn out rather to (his) advantage than otherwise'. He may have been thinking rather of orders for his pottery than of support for his canal; but in promoting the canal he was certainly tireless.

The climax of the negotiations for the Burslemites came at a public meeting in Wolseley Bridge on 30 December 1765. This was the result of Wedgwood's determination to make Earl Gower take their scheme under his patronage. John Stafford, a Macclesfield solicitor, wrote to Samuel Wright of Knutsford and described what happened. Earl Gower, Lord Grey, Walter Bagot, Richard Whitworth and Thomas Gilbert were among those present. Victory went quickly to the Burslemites and the Duke of Bridgewater. Earl Gower presided, and Richard Whitworth put forward his scheme for uniting Liverpool, Hull and Bristol. He introduced the plan for a canal from Winsford Bridge via Checkley to the Trent, and proposed that his scheme for linking the three ports should be adopted. Thomas Gilbert then introduced Brindley's plan for a canal from Wilden Ferry through Staffordshire and Harecastle to the River Mersey. The total cost of this canal was given as £101,000, and without more debate two subscription papers were brought out, one towards defraying the parliamentary expenses and the other towards the 'grand design'. John Stafford remarked that the Duke now appeared to have no intention of building an aqueduct over the Mersey; instead, he intended the Trent & Mersey to join his own canal at Agden. Stafford's comment was bitter: 'A glorious scheme it will be for him if he can draw all the carriage between the two great ports of Liverpool and Hull and a great deal from the interior parts of the country into his canal.' No mention was made at the meeting of the plan for the canal to join the Weaver at Northwich; and there was no reference either to the Macclesfield scheme. 'So contemptible are we,' Stafford observed, 'in the eyes of the great schemers of Staffordshire.' He considered himself 'navigation mad', and was obviously much upset by the decision; but he saw little hope of its being reversed.[42]

From this point onwards the campaign was mainly a parliamentary one. On 7 January 1766 Josiah Wedgwood wrote to Bentley, informing him that 'all the Derbyshire Gentlemen' and 'all the most considerable ones in Staffordshire below Wolseley Bridge' were in favour of their canal. Wedgwood was about to set off for London, and he intended to stop en route at Lichfield to try to prevent applications for branches. John Sparrow and others had met with no opposition from the landowners between the River Dane and Wolseley Bridge; and this lack of opposition went beyond their 'most sanguine expectations'. The greatest battle would be with the Weaver Navigation, which Wedgwood considered would 'die hardest'; and he suggested that the disadvantages of the Weaver should be emphasised, in particular the delay in the salt traffic and the mismanagement of the commissioners.[43]

On 15 January 1766 a petition for the Trent & Mersey Canal was presented to the Commons by landowners, tradesmen and manufacturers of the counties of Lancashire, Cheshire, Staffordshire, Warwickshire, Derbyshire, Leicestershire, Nottinghamshire, Lincolnshire and Yorkshire. This canal was to start 'from the River Trent, at or near Wilden Ferry, to lead to or near Swarkestone and Willington, Whichnor, Rudgley, Stone, and Burslem ... and Lawton and Astbury, and to and over the Rivers Dane and Peover ... and so on to the River Mersey ... whereby an easy Communication will be made between the two great Port Towns of Hull and Liverpool'. Leave to bring in a bill was requested, and the petition was referred to a committee, among whom were Thomas Gilbert and the MPs for all the counties mentioned in the petition.

James Brindley, Josiah Wedgwood and Thomas Bentley gave evidence to the committee. Brindley said that the proposed canal would 'greatly reduce the Price of Carriage'. Josiah Wedgwood referred to the 'large Manufactories in the Neighbourhood of the intended Canal, particularly a great Pottery near Newcastle-under-Lyme'. The raw materials and manufactured goods of that pottery amounted to 10,000 or 12,000 tons per annum; and the canal would reduce the expense of carriage for these by three-quarters. It would have the same effect on goods going to and from the ironworks of Birmingham and Wolverhampton, and on coal which was currently transported 10 or 15 miles by land. Bentley gave further examples of the economies which the canal would produce: the cost of sending goods from Birmingham to Liverpool would be reduced from £4 per ton to 30s per ton, and that of sending goods from Manchester to London from £7 per ton to about £4 10s per ton. John Sparrow informed the committee that £63,000 had already been subscribed towards the canal, and said that he was confident that the whole sum could easily be obtained. Leave was then given to bring in the bill.[44]

A petition had also been presented, on 15 January 1766, in favour of the rival scheme for a canal from Witton Brook to Knutsford, Macclesfield, Stockport and Manchester.[45] The members of the committee to which this petition was referred included Samuel Egerton, who was a cousin of the Duke of Bridgewater. In a report presented on 10 February 1766, the surveyor Hugh Oldham and the engineer John Golborne said that the scheme was 'very practicable' and estimated the expense at £44,000. Leave was given for the bill to be brought in. It was read for a first time on 26 February and for a second time on 3 March.[46]

In a petition dated 18 March 1766, however, a number of 'Gentlemen, Merchants, Manufacturers, Tradesmen and others' living in Manchester, Middlewich, Congleton and Stockport, declared their opposition to the Macclesfield scheme; they preferred the bill to make a canal from Wilden Ferry to the Mersey, and the Duke of Bridgewater's bill to extend his canal from Sale Moor to Stockport. The latter (6 Geo III c 17) received the royal assent on this same day, but the canal was never constructed.

Another petition against the Macclesfield scheme was presented on 24 March 1766 by the landowners and mill-owners in Lancashire and Cheshire who claimed that the proposed canal would harm their estates and interests. On 27 March, despite the opposition, the bill was given its third reading.[47] In April the bill was taken to the Lords, and the Duke of Bridgewater attended every discussion of its proposals. April was the most crucial month for all the canal schemes. On 14 April the Duke petitioned against the Macclesfield scheme; and two petitions from landowners and mill-owners in Lancashire and Cheshire were also considered. On 21 April 1766, the bill was ordered to be brought before a committee in three months' time, but it then disappeared.[48]

The Macclesfield scheme had been supported in a pamphlet, *Seasonable Considerations on a Navigable Canal Intended to be cut from the River Trent, in the County of Derby, to the River Mersey, in the County of Chester*. This pamphlet was produced quickly in April 1766. The Trent & Mersey Canal bill had its third reading in the Commons on 21 April 1766, and the news was greeted with joy in the Potteries.[49] Another pamphlet, *Facts and Reasons*, reiterated the case for the canal. A supplement to the pamphlet in favour of river navigation and the Macclesfield scheme attempted to answer *Facts and Reasons*. This pamphlet, which was hurriedly prepared, vehemently contradicted the assertions about the Weaver and the Trent navigations.

The collapse of the Macclesfield scheme weakened the arguments of the Weaver trustees. The development of Macclesfield was hindered by the lack of a canal, but the Macclesfield Copper Co made use of the Grand Trunk from 1789, when they secured a 21-year lease of a warehouse and crane, situated on the canal, from John Lawton at an annual rent of 2s 6d.[50] The Macclesfield Canal was one of the last British canals to be built, but it was opened eventually in 1831.

Petitions in the Commons for and against the Trent & Mersey Canal were numerous.[51] One of the most important petitions was presented by the Duke of Bridgewater on 12 March 1766. The Duke argued that the Trent & Mersey Canal, instead of terminating as planned 'at or near Runcorn Gap', which was about 2,500yd below Hempstones, the proposed terminus of the Duke's canal, should communicate with the Duke's canal 'at or near a Brook, called Preston Brook, near Preston', and be carried 'from thence by one canal to the R. Mersey at or near Runcorn Gap'; this, he claimed, would make both canals more convenient for the public. The Duke undertook to make the canal from Preston Brook to Runcorn Gap.[52] This petition was very much resented by supporters of the river navigations and of the Macclesfield Canal scheme, as it would mean that the Trent & Mersey Canal would reach the Mersey only through the Bridgewater Canal, and would not join the Weaver Navigation.

The Weaver trustees were unable to influence the form of the

Trent & Mersey Canal bill, which received the royal assent on
14 May 1766. The preamble outlined the course of the canal as in
the first petition: 'from the R. Trent, near Wilden Bridge, below
an ancient ferry called Wilden Ferry, to the R. Mersey, at or near
a certain Place called Runcorn Gap'. The act meant failure for the
trustees, as the Weaver Navigation had been ignored; the canal's
route would divert trade from the Weaver at Middlewich, and at
Anderton the two navigations would be very close to one
another. While the act did not safeguard the tonnage of the
Weaver, however, it did protect their water supply. The canal
proprietors were not allowed to take 'any water out of or from
the River Weaver . . . or out of the River Dane, or the brook
called Wincham Brook, or the Peover Eye, or the brook called
Wade Brook'. The canal was not to cross the Weaver or to pass
through any land lying between Witton Bridge and Wincham
Mill. It was to be constructed on the north side of Witton Common, and was to pass north of the salt works at Anderton. These
concessions were small compensation for the trustees. Their
opposition in Parliament, which had cost £291, had been unsuccessful, as their attempt to make the Weaver the western outlet
had been defeated.[53]

The arguments thus ended in triumph for Josiah Wedgwood
and the Duke of Bridgewater. Professor Willan puts forward a
case for regarding the struggle not as a conflict between rival
interests but as a dispute over 'the relative merits of rivers and
canals as means of communication'. [54] In so far as this interpret-
ation is valid, it can be argued that later developments showed the
proponents of river navigation to have been right. It is hard to
believe, however, that a theoretical commitment to artificial
waterways was a predominant motive either for Josiah Wedgwood or for the Duke of Bridgewater.

The act stated that there were to be two bodies: the Company
of the Proprietors of the Navigation from the Trent to the Mersey,
and the Commissioners of the Navigation. There were 101
proprietors, all of whom were shareholders, and they included
many of the notable figures in the campaign: Earl Gower (10
shares), the Duke of Bridgewater (10), James Brindley (10),
Samuel Garbett (6), Richard Whitworth (5), and John Gilbert (5).
Samuel Egerton had 15 shares, and Josiah Wedgwood took 10½
shares after the act was passed. Each shareholder could take a

minimum of one £200 share or a maximum of 20 shares. They could raise the capital sum of £130,000 by 650 shares of £200, payment of 5 per cent interest on calls being allowed. If the capital proved insufficient, £20,000 capital could be raised from outside subscribers, who would then become proprietors. There were no limitations on dividends. The function of the 816 commissioners named in the act was 'to settle, determine and adjust all questions, matters and differences', which might arise between the proprietors and persons interested in land or water affected by the act. One of the commissioners was Sir Rowland Hill; another twenty-two were connected with the pottery industry.

The executive committee included James Brindley as surveyor-general or chief engineer, Hugh Henshall as clerk to the works, John Sparrow as clerk to the proprietors, Josiah Wedgwood as treasurer, T. Nailor, R. Parrott and T. Bateman as clerks to the commissioners of Cheshire, Staffordshire and Derbyshire, ten representatives of the pottery industry, eight representatives of the landowners, two representatives of Birmingham, and Richard Whitworth. Shareholders were to have a vote for every share they held.

The maximum toll was to be 1½d per ton per mile, but lime and limestone were to pay only one-third of the toll, and paving-stones, gravel, sand for road repairs, soil, marl and manure for land were to pay no toll. The rates were to be fixed by the proprietors, and were to be equal throughout the whole canal. On the Duke of Bridgewater's part of the canal between Preston Brook and the Mersey the rate of toll was to be 1d per ton per mile on coal, stone, timber and other goods, and ½d per ton per mile on limestone. This part of the canal was not to pass within 360yd of Norton Hall, the mansion house of Sir Richard Brook; and this condition was to cause much delay and difficulty for the Duke. The act laid down that milestones were to be erected at the end of each mile.

News of the act was greeted with jubilation at Burslem. On 26 July 1766 the canal was ceremonially begun by Josiah Wedgwood, who cut the first sod below Brownhills. James Brindley was present on this occasion, and many tributes were paid to him. After Wedgwood had cut the first sod, some of the most important people of the district either cut a turf or wheeled a barrow of earth to mark the event. In the afternoon a sheep was roasted whole in Burslem market-place for 'the good of the poorer class of potters'; a bonfire was lit in front of Wedgwood's house, and 'sundry other demonstrations of local rejoicing wound up the day's proceedings'.

It was, as Samuel Smiles said, 'a great day for the Potteries'.[55] A few months after the celebrations Josiah Wedgwood affirmed his confidence in the canal by purchasing Ridge House estate in Shelton, which was intersected by the canal. On the west bank he built his new Etruria works, and to the east of the canal he built Etruria Hall for himself. On each side of the main road between the Fowlea Brook and the canal he built cottages and bakehouses for his workmen.[56]

# 2

# The Construction
# of the Trent & Mersey Canal

The first meeting of the company of proprietors of the canal was held at The Crown in Stone at 11 am on 10 June 1766. John Sparrow was appointed clerk at a salary of £100 per annum; James Brindley, as surveyor-general, was given a salary of £200 per annum; and Hugh Henshall as clerk of the works had a salary of £150 per annum for himself and one clerk. Josiah Wedgwood was honorary treasurer, and a call of £6 per cent was ordered to be made upon the subscribers.

The work was ordered to be begun at both ends of Harecastle tunnel and at Wilden Ferry, and any requests for payment on account of expenses incurred in obtaining the act were to be put before the committee at their next meeting in London on 2 July. Notes on the meeting were sent by Josiah Wedgwood to Thomas Bentley on 12 June, with a message saying, 'I most sincerely congratulate you on the success your labours have again been crown'd with and on the new worlds which are opening to our view.' In an undated letter, probably sent at the end of June 1766, Wedgwood wrote to Bentley about his visit with Henshall to Etruria. He reported that they had been 'setting out the Canal through that district', and added: 'on Monday next, I shall begin to make it'. The ground was 'unfortunately' level, and the canal, in keeping with Brindley's practice, was to run in a straight line through the fields. Wedgwood, who disliked this lack of deviation, referred to Brindley as an 'inflexible Vandal' who would not give 'one *line of Grace*'. Later Wedgwood defended Brindley when he was attacked for having chosen a bad route for the canal through the Etruria estate. Wedgwood had undertaken to make that part himself, on condition that he was not paid for it until the

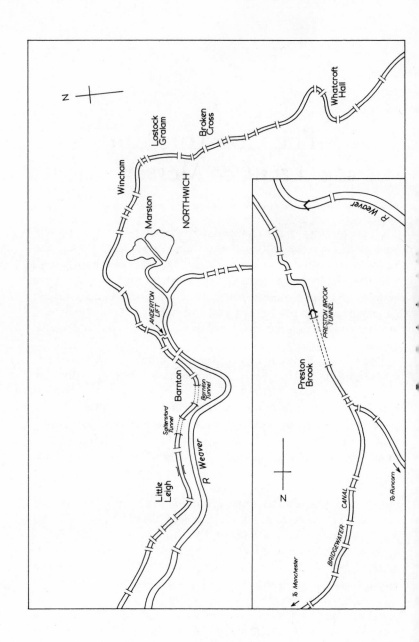

canal was cut on either side. Wedgwood asserted: 'This and other calumnies on Mr. Brindley's character have been industriously spread by a party, who, unless a timely remedy can be applied, are likely to retard our progress, if not to defeat the whole undertaking, and to do more injury than their subscriptions can ever atone for.'[1]

On 18 July 1766 Wedgwood replied to Bentley's inquiry about a proposed canal from Chester to a junction with the Trent & Mersey 'betwixt Wiggan and Runkhorn', with the statement, 'I have not heard anything of the intended navigable canal you mention, but imagine if carried into question it must robb us of a good deal of tonnage.'[2] As a result of the plans for the Trent & Mersey Canal, Chester was in danger of isolation, with trade bypassing the Dee and going via the Trent & Mersey to Liverpool; so in 1770 and 1771 a scheme was proposed for a canal from Chester to Middlewich, joining the Trent & Mersey there, with a branch to Nantwich. The Duke of Bridgewater and the Trent & Mersey Canal Co., however, refused to allow a junction, and laid down conditions that there must be 100yd at Middlewich between the two canals. The Chester Canal Act (12 Geo III c 75) was passed on 1 April 1772, but the canal was not a great success.[3]

Brindley superintended a great many canal works while the Trent & Mersey was being constructed. On 2 March 1767 Wedgwood wrote to Bentley: 'We have several Navigation schemes in embryo, one from the Grand Trunk to Coventry, Banbury and I don't know where, the money was subscribed for survey &c and Mr. Brindley applied to, but he told them they were too precipitate ... he would look over the Country in a year or two if he could.' Wedgwood expressed concern at the effect over-work was having on Brindley's health: 'I am afraid he will do too much and leave us before his vast designs are executed, he is so incessantly harassed on every side that he hath no rest either for his mind or his body and will not be prevailed upon to take care of his health ... for I think Brindley, *The Great*, The fortunate, money-getting Brindley an object of pity.' Wedgwood again referred to Brindley's health on 2 April, and to the fact that he was going to Buxton for a few weeks. Wedgwood hoped this would have 'a good effect upon his constitution as his ailments certainly proceed from a too intense and constant application to business both with body and mind'.

The General Assembly for 1767 was held in April at Stone, which became the headquarters of the Company, and the Duke of Bridgewater and Earl Gower attended .The atmosphere seemed very harmonious, and Earl Gower humorously told the proprietors that they should be styled the 'Amicable Society of Navigators'. A plan to dig the canal by means of ploughs had proved abortive, and a deviation of the line of the canal was accepted in order that the canal might be carried over rock-salt mines at Lawton. The Navigation committee expressed satisfaction, in September, at the progress of the canal, and Brindley went so far as to assert that it would be completed 'in five years from Christmas next', being prepared to bet £200 on this claim. On 24 June 1768 Sir Randle Wilbraham of Rode Hall was paid £30 an acre for 13 chains 84 links of land.[4]

The tunnels were five in number: Harecastle 2,880yd, Preston Brook 1,239yd, Barnton 572yd, Saltersford 424yd and Armitage (originally Hermitage) 130yd. Of these only Armitage had a towpath, the earliest example of this. Harecastle was begun on 27 July 1766, but it took longer to complete than had been expected because the geological conditions were more difficult than those Brindley had encountered in constructing the underground canal system at Worsley. At the northern end of the tunnel there was quicksand, and this was succeeded by the hard rocks known as millstone grit and Rowley rag. As on the Bridgewater Canal, side-tunnels or drifts were excavated to the workings of a nearby colliery, and water draining through them from this colliery was used to supply the summit.[5]

Harecastle was the first tunnel of its kind, and had many defects. It was only 12ft high and 9ft wide, and a narrow boat had to be propelled through the tunnel by legging. There developed a special class of 'leggers' who had a shelter near the tunnel entrance. The tunnel was unlighted and the leggers lay on their backs in the darkness, on legging-boards laid across the boat; they propelled the boat along by pushing with their feet against the top or sides of the tunnel. The other tunnels were 17ft 4in high and 13½ft wide.[6]

Sir Joseph Banks (1743–1820), the famous botanist who made a journey through Wales and the Midlands in 1767–8 looking for rare plants and shrubs, commented unfavourably on the quality of the mortar being used in the early stages of the construction of

Harecastle tunnel. At the time of his visit, first to Burslem and then to Harecastle, about 100yd of the tunnel had been dug. He described it as 'well arched and nobly siz'd', but added: 'their mortar is so soft and seems to have so little care taken in making it, that I cannot help having my fears of accidents which may befall it when it comes to bear a large weight of hill'.

John Rennie, reporting to the Trent & Mersey proprietors on 11 September 1820, commented on the poor workmanship at Harecastle: 'In many places the roof is not more than 6 feet above the ordinary level of the water, in others it's $6\frac{1}{2}$, 7, $7\frac{1}{2}$ and 8 feet, in some places it is too narrow, in others crooked.' Rennie said that the brickwork on the bottom, sides and top of the tunnel was not more than 9 inches thick, and it had 'throughout been made with bad mortar'. He described the results as follows: 'In all the brickwork under water, and wherever there is springs or moisture that keeps it damp, the mortar is as soft as clay, the bricks in many places can therefore be pulled out with little labour and in the low parts of the roof and in some of the projecting parts of the sides, the Brickwork is worn away by the rubbing of the Boats and their Cargoes to nearly half its thickness.' Rennie also commented on the bad condition of the side-tunnels which communicated with the various coal works. He concluded that the tunnel was in several parts 'too narrow and low', and that from 'long experience' it had been found 'quite inadequate for the business transacted'.[7]

A less critical account had been offered in *Aris's Birmingham Gazette* on 5 September 1767:

> Gentlemen come to view our Eighth Wonder of the World – the subterraneous Navigation which is cutting by the great Mr. Brindley who handles Rocks as easily as you would Plumb-Pyes and makes the four elements subservient to his will. He is as plain a looking man as one of his own Carters, but when he speaks all Ears listen, and every Mind is filled with Wonder at the things he pronounces to be practicable. He has cut a mile through Bogs, which he binds up, embanking them with Stones which he gets out of other Parts of the Navigation, besides about a quarter of a Mile into the Hill Yelden, on the side of which he has a pump, which is worked by Water, and a Stove, the Fire of which sucks through a Pipe the Damps that

would annoy the Men who are cutting toward the Centre of the Hill. The clay he cuts out, serves for bricks to arch the sub-terranean Part, which we heartily wish to see finished to Wilden Ferry, when we shall be able to send Coals and Pots to London and to different parts of the Globe.[8]

On 6 October 1768 the *Derby Mercury* gave an account of a General Assembly of the proprietors of the Trent & Mersey Canal which had been held at Wolseley Bridge on 29 September. It was reported that 22 miles of the navigation had been completed and that '409 yards of the subterraneous Passage at Harecastle was cut and vaulted, besides the vast Openings at each Entrance'. The committee expressed confidence in the progress of the work, saying that 14 locks, 26 bridges and 6 boats had been built. It was also stated that the canal was made navigable over the River Trent at Wychnor 'without the Assistance of a Bridge or Acquaduct'.[9] At Alrewas lock the canal flows into the Trent for 200yd, and passes dangerously near to a large weir. Beyond the weir the canal crosses the water meadows to the fourteenth-century Wychnor Church. Sluices and weirs carry water from the naviga-tion to the Trent, and at Wychnor lock the Trent leaves the navigation.[10]

Arthur Young visited Harecastle about 1768, and in his *Tour Through the North of England* he declared that the tunnel was 'cer-tainly an amazing work'. He described the fifteen shafts which were sunk from the hill-top at different places to reach the level of the intended canal, the horse-gins which were used to draw up the earth, rock and coal and the windmills which worked pumps to draw up the water.[11] These windmills were able to cope with small amounts of water, but as the excavations penetrated further into the hill, vast quantities were encountered and the 'miners were often drowned out'. A steam-engine or 'fire-engine' was therefore placed at the top of the hill to pump out this volume of water; in fact, it is possible that more than one engine was used. The excavation proceeded from both ends at once, and when the whole line of the excavation was united by a continuous tunnel, the water ran out at both ends and the steam-engine could be dispensed with.

John Phillips, the surveyor and writer on waterways, claimed in the fourth edition of his history of inland navigation, published in 1803, that he had been engaged on the operation of making the tunnel: 'I was at the digging and vaulting the first tunnel that ever was performed in the country, invented by my old master Mr. Brindley, through Harecastle, in Staffordshire in 1776, and which cost £3 10s 8d per yard, and that was thought a great sum of money.'[12] On 13 July 1772 it was announced in *Aris's Birmingham Gazette* that Harecastle tunnel was now open 'for more than a mile on one side of the hill and above half a mile on the other and that the rest will soon be completed'.

Despite the opposition of some of the Trent & Mersey's proprietors, Josiah Wedgwood was anxious that a canal should be made to Coventry. The act (8 Geo III c 36) was passed on 29 January 1768; it provided for a canal from the Grand Trunk at Fradley via Huddlesford, Fazeley, Atherstone and Nuneaton to Coventry. James Brindley was appointed engineer and surveyor at a salary of £150 per annum; but in September 1769 he was dismissed, because of dissatisfaction with the progress of the work. The chief aim of the canal was to supply Coventry with cheap coal. In April 1769 the Oxford Canal Co obtained an act to join the Coventry line at Longford and construct a canal to Oxford.[13] Josiah Wedgwood wrote in January 1769 to Sampson Lloyd of Coventry: 'We look upon your Canal, the Oxford, and any other which may join with that and point towards the Metropolis, as so many extensions of the Grand Trunk ... we therefore wish to have the Great and public Road made as straight, easy and commodious as may be'.[14]

In the House of Commons on 27 February 1770 Sir John Wrottesley, MP for Staffordshire, presented the report of a committee which had been considering the application of the Trent & Mersey Co for authority to raise more capital. James Brindley gave his account of the canal: 40 miles 'open work' was completed, '33 from Hock Hill towards Wilden Ferry, 4½ on both sides of Hare Castle, and 2¾ miles on each side of Preston Hill'. Of the Harecastle tunnel 944yd were completed, and of the Preston tunnel 125yd. Other works completed included 21 locks, 60 road bridges, 13 boats, and 50 culverts or arches for carrying brooks and rivers under the canal. The lock below Swarkestone was nearly finished; and Brindley estimated that the whole of the navigation would be finished in '3 years from Christmas last'. John Sparrow said that £86,900 had been paid to the treasurer, and that almost all of that sum had been expended. As the calls were made, he said, the proprietors would subscribe £43,100 making a total of £130,000. Sparrow considered that £50,000 more than the £150,000 allowed them in the original act would be needed to complete the navigation, and this was granted.

At the same time, however, amendments to the original act were requested. These amendments would enable the proprietors to take tonnages for distances less than a mile; would make the transfer of shares easier; and would define the maximum length and burden for vessels passing through locks. On 28 March 1770 it was reported that all the amendments except one had been agreed to and that two other clauses had been added: one of these would compel people to shut swivel-bridges, and the others would authorise an agreement with Lord Paget, the owner of the Trent Navigation from Wilden Ferry to Burton, for water to be taken out of the Trent. The bill was given the royal assent on 12 April 1770.[15]

On 9 March 1770 the Duke of Bridgewater presented a petition to the Commons concerning a clause in the act of 1766 which restrained him from making his canal within 360yd of Norton Hall. The Duke argued that the nature of the ground and the springs made it impossible to build a canal of the necessary depth under the restrictions prescribed. His petition encountered strong opposition. Sir Richard Brook, the heir of an old-established family which had acquired Norton Priory when the monasteries were dissolved, was resolved to defend his property against the workmen who would build the canal and the boatmen who would use it. What Hugh Malet calls 'the Battle of Norton Priory' was a costly and difficult business for the Duke. There was no possibility of diverting the canal round the Norton Hall estate because the junction with the Trent & Mersey at Preston Brook was too far south to make this practicable. In desperation, the Duke ordered the canal to be started at Runcorn, and a flight of ten locks, built by John Gilbert to take boats down to the port, was completed in January 1773. This meant that Sir Richard had the canal at each end of his land, with public opinion much in favour of the navigation's completion. Finally, at the beginning of 1776, he allowed the canal to go through his estate, and accepted £1,900 as compensation. By 21 March 1776 the Duke's canal was completed from Manchester to Liverpool and was ready to exchange traffic with the Trent & Mersey.[16]

The Trent & Mersey Co announced that their canal would be finished and opened for traffic from Derwent Mouth to Shugborough in Staffordshire on 24 June 1770. Applications for the carriage of goods were to be made to Hugh Henshall, or to Joseph Smith, wharfinger in Gainsborough.[17] In September 1770 it was announced that the canal was open for traffic from Great Haywood (the junction with the Staffordshire & Worcestershire Canal, then nearing completion) to the River Trent at Weston. In order that 'quick and uniform Dispatch' might be ensured, vessels were to 'set out from Great Haywood on every Monday and Thursday Mornings at Six o'clock, and arrive at Weston on the Tuesday and Friday Nights following'. Warehouses had been built at Great Haywood, Bromley Common and Weston, and wharfingers were stationed at these places.[18] On 12 November 1771 the canal was opened to Stone, and two boats laden with flint and clay arrived there. The canal was forced to close temporarily, however, after the repeated firing of a cannon in celebration had caused a lock and bridge to collapse; the repairs cost £1,000.[19]

By this time the Trent & Mersey Canal Co had adopted its motto. In an undated letter, probably written in March 1768, Josiah Wedgwood sent Thomas Bentley the version of the motto usually quoted, *Pro patriam populumque fluit*. This is commonly translated as, 'It flows for the land and the people'; but this version of the motto seems to be linguistically corrupt. Since the preposition *pro* is normally followed by the ablative case, one would expect it to read *Pro patria populoque fluit*. Wedgwood also sent two sketches of the proposed seal, commenting: 'Below is the motto and I believe the seal is intended to be somehow as below, but have not in the least concerned myself about it as there are so many abler heads in the committee.' The first sketch had the motto round the circumference, and a boat in the centre, with lines underneath to indicate water and the words 'Navigation from the Trent to the Mersey'. The second had these words round the circumference and 'a boat . . . perhaps drawn by a horse' in the centre, with the motto underneath the lines indicating water.

If one looks at Plate 1 of Charles Hadfield's *The Canals of the West Midlands* (David & Charles, 1969), one finds a very clear photograph of the company's seal, which was used as an etched relief on the Wedgwood bicentenary commemorative goblet. Round the circumference of the seal are the words 'Company of the Proprietors of the Navigation from the Trent to the Mersey', and in the centre is a splendid picture of a sunny day in the Potteries, with a horse pulling a loaded vessel along a waterway. The implication, clearly, is that the canal will bring prosperity to Staffordshire; and under the picture is the motto, *In patriam populumque fluat*. Literally, this means, 'May it flow into the fatherland and the people'; and it seems at least to be grammatical Latin. An attempt to establish the origin of this motto, however, leads to the surprising conclusion that it must be adapted from a stanza in one of Horace's political odes. In the sixth ode of Book III, Horace laments the corruption of moral standards in ancient Rome:

> *fecunda culpae saecula nuptias*
> *primum inquinavere et genus et domos:*
>    *hoc fonte derivata clades*
>     *in patriam populumque fluxit.*

C. E. Bennett in the Loeb edition translates as follows:

> Teeming with sin, our times have sullied first the marriage-bed, our offspring, and our homes; sprung from this source, disaster's stream has overflowed the folk and fatherland.

The motto shown on the canal seal is the last line of this stanza, with the perfect indicative *fluxit* replaced by the present subjunctive *fluat*. The natural and idiomatic translation, it would appear, is something like 'May it flood the countryside and drown the population'. It seems an odd motto for a canal company, but fortunately it had little effect on the canal's history.

On 23 November 1768 the Mayor of Liverpool reported that he had received a letter from the proprietors of the Trent & Mersey Canal in which they informed him of a meeting to be held at Trentham on 29 November 'concerning carrying on or continuing the said Navigation by a Bridge Aqueduct and path or road from Runcorn over the Mersey to Liverpool, and also from the said Staffordshire Canal to Chester'. Representatives of the corporation were invited to attend the meeting and hear whether the Duke would join his canal to this proposed navigation, and James Brindley was to be asked to survey the proposed canal route, and to estimate its cost and that of building the bridge.[20] Brindley's support for the scheme, however, began to weaken when disputes developed about the widening of the western section between Preston Brook and Middlewich; he felt that the construction of a large-scale aqueduct over the Mersey might present insuperable problems. In July 1769 Wedgwood wrote to Bentley: 'The advocates for a wide Tunnel (at Preston Brook) say that salt cannot be transhipped if the labour of doing it could be got for nothing, therefore we must either have a wide Tunnel, a Bridge at Runcorn, or carry no Salt to Liverpool. The wide Tunnel therefore is continued till we see the probability of a bridge as we cannot think of giving up the salt trade.'

The broad section was built, at an extra cost of £20,000; but the canal did not get its aqueduct, mainly because the Duke opposed it. The Weaver trustees benefited from this, since the Weaver and the Mersey continued to carry the Liverpool salt trade; but their cheapness would probably have secured that trade to them, even if the aqueduct had been built. The Duke of Bridgewater's barges proved too wide for the canal from Preston Brook to Middlewich, so despite the expense of widening this section goods had to be transhipped from broad to narrow boats at Preston Brook.[21]

Etruria Hall was completed for Josiah Wedgwood in 1770. The house faced towards the Etruria works, which were about 300yd away. The intervening area was landscaped, with ornamental grounds leading to two small lakes near the canal. As a result of the gradual growth of the Shelton ironworks, after 1858, the garden and park around the hall disappeared.[22] As early as 1767, Wedgwood was consulting with Bentley about branches to the works. On 31 December 1767 he wrote: 'My present thoughts are to make the Canal opposite the works wide enough for a boat to lye to the side of the Canal without interrupting the Navigation, by which means every material will be taken out of the boat opposite to that part of the works where it is wanted – which could not be done by a single branch.'[23] The canal, which bounded the works on the east, was widened to form lay-bys; and two branches were taken into the works.[24]

On 27 September 1772 James Brindley died. He had been surveying a branch canal between Leek and Froghall, and had got drenched near Ipstones. Brindley had remained some time in his wet clothing; to make matters worse he had slept in a damp bed at the Ipstones inn, with the result that he became seriously ill, diabetes aggravating the chill. He died in his house at Turnhurst, near Golden Hill, and was buried nearby at Newchapel. He and his young wife Anne, the sister of Hugh Henshall, had lived at Turnhurst since their marriage on 8 December 1765; the house was demolished in 1929.

Samuel Smiles called Brindley 'probably one of the most remarkable instances of self-taught genius to be found in the whole range of biography'. [25] The *Gentleman's Magazine* had described him, in January 1766, as 'one of those great geniuses which nature sometimes rears by her own force, and brings to maturity without the necessity of cultivation'. In October 1772 the same magazine noted his death, describing him as 'the celebrated engineer, who projected the Duke of Bridgewater's navigation'.[26] Brindley had surveyed and planned seven navigations in addition to the Duke's, and had been consulted on numerous other projects, such as the Leeds and Liverpool Canal and the improvement of the Thames Navigation to Reading. Despite his failure at times to keep pace with the demands made on him, his achievement in solving many of the new problems connected with inland navigation identifies him beyond doubt as a great man.

He was succeeded, in accordance with a wish expressed on his death-bed, by Hugh Henshall. In a letter of October 1772, which survives in draft form, Josiah Wedgwood told Sir Roger Newdigate that Henshall's 'knowledge in mechanicks, unwearied industry, and the strictest integrity' rendered him well-qualified to complete the canal, which was now open from 'the Trent to the Pottery'. Wedgwood added that they were 'very anxious to have the Coventry and Oxford Canals finished that Land Carriage may be totally abolish'd betwixt us and London'.[27]

On 29 September 1772 the report of the committee to the General Assembly stated that 48 miles of the canal had 'for some time' been navigable, and that '27 boats belonging to the Company and 11 to other persons' were in use. It was expected that the length from Stone to Stoke would be navigable in about two weeks. There were 10 company boats employed on the Trent between Wilden Ferry and Gainsborough: 40 locks, 112 cartbridges, 9 foot-bridges, 117 culverts, 1,946yd of Harecastle tunnel and 738yd of Preston Brook tunnel had been completed, £130,000 had been subscribed, and an additional sum of £28,650 had been borrowed. The stock of the company, consisting of boats, stone, timber, lime, bricks and other materials, amounted to £10,323. The total revenue from tonnage from 29 September 1771 to 5 September 1772 amounted to £2,882, with a profit on freight carrying of £575 by the canal boats and of £515 by the boats on the Trent. On 14 November 1772, in a letter to Edward Sneyd of Lichfield, John Sparrow expressed his confidence that profits would be increased in a short time. Samuel Egerton of Tatton Park had undertaken to lend money to the company, and this was used to pay debts, to carry on the works, and to pay annual interest to the proprietors.[28] The Egertons' house dominated the Cheshire village of Knutsford, the 'Cranford' of Mrs Gaskell's novel.

In April 1773 it was reported that 66 miles of the navigation were 'entirely finished', that the canal from Wilden Ferry to Stoke had been navigable 'for some Time', and that 'many Vessels' had used it. The 'magnificent' aqueducts over the Rivers Dove and Trent were completed, and the 'Whole of this great and useful Undertaking was carrying on with the utmost Success'.[29] The aqueduct with twenty-three stone arches carried the canal across the River Dove south of Egginton, and was approached on each side by an embankment 1 mile and 2 furlongs in length. The aqueduct over the Trent near Rugeley had six arches of 21ft each.[30]

The Duke of Bridgewater, attended by the agents of the Trent & Mersey Co, was able to sail 'near a measured Mile' into the Harecastle tunnel on 1 November 1773; and he expressed 'great Satisfaction at that wonderful Work of Art'. Boats were already being loaded with coal from a side-tunnel, and its price was reported to be 3s 6d per ton.[31] The general account for the year 1773 showed that £176,217 had been spent on the canal; this included £3,239 on boats and equipment and £1,481 on goods in stock. The sum of £129,400 had been raised by 647 shares; £47,480 had been raised on the credit of the tolls; net tonnage amounted to £2,247; net profit on the freight was £417; profit on coal was £34; and interest on stock was £120.[32]

In 1773 the idea of a branch canal from the summit level to Leek was under discussion. On 23 January 1773 Josiah Wedgwood wrote to Bentley about a bill which John Sparrow was to promote for this purpose. The canal was to be only 12ft wide, and was to have inclined planes instead of locks. The boats would carry 5 tons each, and the principal cargoes would be coal, lime and stone.[33] John Sneyd (1734–1809), landowner and botanist, was interested in this idea; and in a letter to Sir Joseph Banks he described the aim of the canal and gave details of the inclined plane:

> Great improvements are making in ye moorlands which will raise ye value of all our Estates. The principle Roads are already as good as any in England, and we are going to petition Parliament for a navigable Canal from ye Pottery beyond Leek principally for Coal and Lime Carriage which [can] be executed at a very moderate Expense by means of an Invention one of our Moorlanders has hit off for drawing loaded Barges of 7 or 8 Tons up an inclined plane which rises 13 inches in ye yard instead of Locks. This has been tryed out at large and a boy of 12 years old draws them up with ye greatest ease by a common Capstan. The Boat swims over a 4 wheeled Carriage which sinks to ye bottom of ye Canal, it is then fasten'd upon it and so drawn over. The Capstan should be fixt at ye summit.

Despite the phrase 'tryed at large', this ingenious idea was not adopted until later; and the canal scheme was not then carried out. On 14 November 1793 the *Derby Mercury* stated that the supporters of the 'Froghall Canal' had prevented the building of a canal to Leek.[34] Plans were made, too, for a connection between the Trent & Mersey near Burton and the Breedon limestone works. On 22 November 1773, Josiah Wedgwood told Bentley that he had met Lord Stamford, the owner of the works, to discuss a branch canal for the transporting of coal and lime, but this plan came to nothing.[35]

The construction of the canal from Middlewich to Preston Brook presented Hugh Henshall with serious engineering difficulties. On 11 September 1774 Wedgwood wrote to Bentley about a proposed visit to this section, where the track in places approached 'as near to impracticability as anything can do which is really to be executed'. On 19 September Wedgwood wrote to Bentley that they had reached Sandbach on the first day, and that there were about twenty-seven locks to finish and two more tunnels to make before the navigation would be completed. The tunnels were Saltersford and Barnton; they were needed because of the difficulty of building the canal along the north side of the

Weaver valley where the steep slope caused landslides. As Wedgwood explained: 'Mr. Henshall deeming it impractical to make the Canal along the high sloping banks of the Weaver, has cut out these new Tunnels, and very happy it is for us that the ground has been found capable of admitting this alternative, or I verily believe we must have given up this part of our Canal, and even now we have some tremendous Gullies and sidelong banks to pass over, but none I hope impracticable'.[36]

In Shaw's 'Tour to the West of England' the tunnels of the Trent & Mersey are described. The most southerly, at Hermitage or Armitage, was 'gazed at with astonishment'. Shaw described Harecastle as lined and arched with brick except towards the centre where about 500yd of solid rock had been blown up with gunpowder. He saw the tunnel soon after its completion, when pleasure-boats were taking sightseers to admire the 'great wonder'. He described his own visit as follows:

> The procession was solemn; some enlivened this scene with a band of musick, but we had none; as we entered far, the light of the candles was necessary, and about half-way, the view back upon the mouth, was like the glimmering of a star, very beautiful. The various voices of the workmen from the mines, &c, were rude and aweful, and to be present at their quarrels, which sometimes happen when they meet, and battle for a passage, must resemble greatly the ideas we may form of the regions of Pluto.[37]

On 7 March 1775 the parliamentary committee examining another petition from the Trent & Mersey reported on the progress of the canal. Hugh Henshall gave evidence that about 75 miles were completed, and claimed that 'the great Tunnel through Harecastle Hill of the length of about 2,900 yards' was made. There were still 15 miles to be completed: £130,000 had been raised and £68,550 had been borrowed at 4½ per cent, but no interest on calls had been paid for four years. Permission was given to bring in a bill to allow the company to raise more money. On 13 April 1775 the royal assent was given to an act (15 Geo III c 20) to enable them to raise £75,000.

By September, the canal was navigable for 77½ miles, and 82 miles were completed, There were 163 cart-bridges, 11 footbridges, 72 locks and 155 culverts. The proprietors had advanced

£130,000 and £105,430 had been borrowed on the credit of the undertaking. From these sums, the money received for freight and tonnage, and the interest on money advanced, the company had expended £240,219; the sum remaining in the treasurer's hands was £4,250. The net income from tonnage from 31 March 1770, when the first part of the canal was opened, to 2 September 1775 was £20,532; £3,882 of this had been earned in the last six months of that period.[38]

In March 1776 Edward Sneyd of Woodstanton, who held twenty-one shares in the Trent & Mersey Canal Co, wrote a poem, 'On the Navigable Canal', in which he celebrated the progress that the canal had brought:

> The rustling canvas now with pomp conveys
> The precious traffic of this favor'd isle:
> The dreary wastes are now supply'd with corn
> From foreign parts, where meagre famine reign'd:
> See wharfs commodious range along the shore,
> The publick granges of a freeborn state.

Sneyd paid tribute to the canal's engineer:

> And, rous'd by sad remembrance, shed a tear
> O'er Brindley's urn, whose relicks are consign'd
> By Death relentless, to the realms of night.
> May endless bliss attend his hallow'd stride,
> The matchless artist of this fair canal.

Josiah Wedgwood responded to this eulogy with amusement: 'What a country you have painted. Even our dirty tiny canal no sooner becomes the subject of your creative Muse, than its stagnant ochery surface, which before reminded us of the plagues of Egypt, becomes a gentle current – a glassy stream – with flowery banks – ha – ha – ha!'[39]

The opening of a canal was often the occasion for lavish celebrations, and the committee of management sometimes made a ceremonial journey along part of the route. No record of such celebrations has survived in the case of the Trent & Mersey Canal; but D. P. Davies, in a *History of Derbyshire* published in 1811, states that Henshall 'put the last hand to it in May 1777'. The fall in the Winsford tonnage in that year confirms this date:[40]

| Year | Tons |
|------|------|
| 1776–7 | 13,917 |
| 1777–8 | 9,760 |
| 1778–9 | 6,068 |
| 1779–80 | 5,284 |

On 21 July 1777 Hugh Henshall & Co, carriers, whose carrying business was run by some of the proprietors of the Trent & Mersey, announced the opening of the canal and gave carriage rates. They compared the cost per ton for various distances by canal and by land:[41]

| Between | Canal | | | Land | | |
|---------|-------|---|---|------|---|---|
|  | £ | s | d | £ | s | d |
| Gainsbro' and Birmingham | 1 | 10 | 0 | — | | |
| Manchester and Etruria | | 15 | 0 | 2 | 15 | 0 |
| Manchester and Lichfield (including road to canal) | 1 | 2 | 6 | 4 | 0 | 0 |
| Manchester and Derby (road to Shardlow) | 1 | 15 | 0 | 3 | 0 | 0 |
| Manchester and Leicester (road to Shardlow) | 2 | 6 | 8 | 6 | 0 | 0 |
| Manchester and Shardlow | 1 | 10 | 0 | — | | |
| Manchester and Nottingham | 2 | 0 | 0 | 4 | 0 | 0 |
| Manchester and Newark | 2 | 0 | 0 | 5 | 6 | 8 |
| Manchester and Wolverhampton | 1 | 5 | 0 | 4 | 13 | 4 |
| Manchester and Birmingham | 1 | 10 | 0 | 4 | 0 | 0 |
| Manchester and Stourport | 1 | 10 | 0 | 4 | 13 | 4 |
| Manchester and Stourport for wool, hops and bulky articles | 1 | 10 | 0 | — | | |
| Liverpool and Etruria | | 13 | 4 | 2 | 10 | 0 |
| Liverpool and Bromley Common (for Lichfield) | 1 | 0 | 0 | — | | |
| Liverpool and Shardlow | 1 | 10 | 0 | — | | |
| Liverpool and Notts and Newark | 2 | 0 | 0 | — | | |
| Liverpool and Wolverhampton | 1 | 5 | 0 | 5 | 0 | 0 |
| Liverpool and Birmingham | 1 | 10 | 0 | 5 | 0 | 0 |
| Liverpool and Stourport | 1 | 10 | 0 | 5 | 0 | 0 |
| Chester and Wolverhampton | 1 | 15 | 0 | 3 | 10 | 0 |
| Chester and Birmingham and Stourport | 2 | 0 | 0 | 3 | 10 | 0 |

The length of the canal was 93⅜ miles. There were 213 bridges,

2 Middlewich and Kidsgrove

only one of which, at Weston Cliff, was of stone. The rise of the canal from Preston Brook to Harecastle was 326ft, and the fall from Harecastle to Derwent Mouth was 316ft. Originally, there were 35 locks on the northern side of Harecastle and 40 on the southern side. Under an act of 1809 (49 Geo III c 73) however, a staircase of 3 locks at Lawton was reconstructed as 4 separate locks; and thereafter there were 36 locks on the northern side. In the original construction, the canal was 29ft wide at the top, 16ft wide at the bottom, and 4½ft deep. The locks were 7ft wide, and were adapted for boats 70 to 74ft long, 6ft 8in to 6ft 10in wide, and of about 25 tons burden. From Wilden Ferry to Burton-on-Trent and from Middlewich to Preston Brook, however, the canal was 31ft wide at the top, 18ft wide at the bottom, and 5½ft deep; and the locks were 14ft wide, being intended for river barges of 40 tons burden.[42] The narrow dimensions of the central section were designed to save both water and money. As it was, the canal cost £296,600. Wedgwood wrote to R. L. Edgeworth on 13 February 1786: 'I cannot give you any satisfactory account of the price of cutting our canal per mile. The whole length of the canal is 94 miles and it has cost to complete it near £300,000 but I suppose the mere cutting of a mile of our canal would not cost more than £700 or £800.'

Much of the capital came from the landowners of the area who contributed £141,100; £46,750 of this came from Samuel Egerton. London was the centre of the promotion campaign, and £56,000 was raised there. Lichfield, although it did not get its branch canal, subscribed £46,500. The Potteries, where the main concern was in cheap transport rather than in dividends, had, in 1782, contributed £19,300, or 5 per cent of the share and loan capital. There were no shareholders in Hull or Birmingham, although subscription books had been opened there, and only one shareholder came from Liverpool. Thomas Bentley had no shares, Erasmus Darwin only one; and Wedgwood took ten and a half shares after the act had been obtained.[43]

The canal stimulated economic growth, particularly in the Potteries, in a relatively short time. When John Wesley first visited Burslem in 1760, the potters hurled clods of earth at him and his congregation. When he returned in 1781, Wesley was amazed to find 'the whole face of the country changed in about twenty years'. Inhabitants had 'flowed in from every side', villages and towns had grown up, and the 'wilderness' had become 'a fruitful field'.[44]

In 1782 Thomas Pennant, the traveller, described the great benefits the canal had brought to the area through which it passed:

> Notwithstanding the clamours which have been raised against this undertaking, in the places through which it was intended to pass, when it was first projected, we have the pleasure now to see content reign universally on its banks, and plenty attend its progress. The cottage, instead of being half-covered with miserable thatch, is now secured with a substantial covering of tiles or slates, brought from the distant hills of Wales or Cumberland. The fields, which before were barren, are now drained, and by the assistance of manure, conveyed on the canal toll-free, are clothed with a beautiful verdure. Places which rarely knew the use of coal, are plentifully supplied with that essential article upon reasonable terms; and what is still of greater utility, the monopolizers of corn are prevented from exercising their infamous trade.

Pennant considered that the completion of the canal had resulted in prosperity for the country as well as wealth for the shareholders.[45]

The populace, however, still lived precariously, and a poor harvest could still cause local scarcity. This happened in March 1783, as this extract from a letter written in Newcastle-under-Lyme shows:

> The people in the Pottery of this Town are in a State of absolute Anarchy; on Friday last a Boat Load of Flour and Cheese, going up the Navigation to Manchester, was seized by a mob of about 400 persons; they opened the Hatches, kept possession of it all Night, and on Saturday proceeded to sell the Flour &c at their own prices. An Express had been sent to Lichfield, to obtain some of the Militia who were quartered there, to come to our relief: Two Companies were accordingly dispatched, and Mr. Inge, Dr. Faulkner, and Major Sneyd, with the utmost Politeness and Alacrity, came here. On Saturday Afternoon, there happening to be a Company of the Caernarvonshire Militia in Town, on their Route homewards, the Commanding Officer, in the most obliging Manner, complied with the

Request of the Magistrates, to assist them in Case of Need. The Magistrates, Military, and many of the most respectable Inhabitants of this Town, immediately went down to Etruria, near Mr. Wedgwood's Manufactory (where the Mob still kept the Boat) determined to quell and disperse them. The Military were kept at some distance from the Spot, in order that an opportunity might be given to reason with the Persons assembled; and the Magistrates and others had the Satisfaction of seeing, that, in a short Time, they yielded to Reason; and being promised all the Assistance that the Law could give against the Forestallers and others, that kept up the Markets, and that a Subscription would be entered into, to obviate the present Scarcity, as far as they could; they agreed to disperse, provided the Boat was not removed.

But on Monday they assembled again in greater Numbers, and sent Deputies to the Magistrates with a written Requisition of what they would have done; in fine, they grew so ill-behaved, that, though there was a very liberal Subscription entered into, [and] they had all the Assurances of Redress and other Assistance that the Magistrates, the Gentlemen present, and their Masters could give them, they would not disperse without the Boat was fully delivered to them on the Instant, that the Flour might be sold there; the Magistrates not chusing, out of Humanity, to go to Extremities, by which there would have been much Bloodshed, thought it best to comply; and so the Mob are now selling the Flour at their own Prices; but, at the same Time, the Gentlemen are determined to prosecute the Ringleaders, to the utmost Rigour of the Law. Two of the Ringleaders are taken and committed to Stafford Gaol.[46]

# 3

# The
# Construction of the Branches

On 14 November 1775 Josiah Wedgwood made one of the earliest references to the possibility of connecting the Trent & Mersey to the lime quarries at Caldon Low. He wrote to Bentley: 'They have enlisted me here in another Navigation scheme, to effect a junction between Caldon Lime Quarries and our Canal and Collieries. You know the Plan, I only mean that we are begun upon it in earnest.'[1] The Earl of Shrewsbury was the owner of the Caldon Low lime quarries; and when the canal was begun, he granted a long lease of them to John Gilbert of Worsley, Sampson Whieldon of Caldon, George Smith of Eaves in Whiston, and Richard Hill of Farley, who were called the Caldon Lime Co. They also had leases of coal measures near Froghall.[2]

On 27 November 1775 John Sparrow wrote to Charles Bill of Marlborough about the proposed canal:

A Plan has long been in Agitation for extending a Branch of the Canal, from the Summit at Harecastle, to an inexhaustible fund of Limestone near Caldon in Staffordshire. Surveys have been made of various courses for this purpose, and at last a very eligible one has been discovered, the length of which is 19¼ miles. An accurate estimate has been made of the expence, which amounts to £23,126. The Committee are perfectly satisfied of the utility of this extention, as well with regard to the Public as the Proprietors of the Trunk Navigation, who are in particular manner interested in promoting it, not only on account of the advantage that may arise from it, in a commercial view, but by the plentiful supply of water it will afford to the Summit at Harecastle, which the numerous Locks there stand in need of.

Sparrow ended by saying that the money would be raised by shares of £200 each.[3]

On 12 February 1776 the proprietors of the Trent & Mersey Canal submitted a petition to Parliament concerning the Caldon branch. The petition referred to 'proper Surveys lately taken', by which it appeared that the branch could be made from the south side of Harecastle via Hanley and Norton to Cheddleton. From there a 'railed Way' could be made for the carriage of coal, stone and other goods from the canal to a place called 'the Sharpcliffe', and from there the canal could be continued to 'several Lime-works and Limestone Quarries at or near Caldon'. By this means 'the Conveyance of Coals, Lime, Limestone, Timber, and other Goods, Wares, and Merchandizes' would be facilitated and rendered less expensive.[4]

A petition against the proposed branch canal was lodged on 19 March 1776 by John Bagnall, Benjamin Yardley and William Adams, owners of water-driven corn-mills at Cheddleton, Milton and Bucknall in Staffordshire, and by 'several Gentlemen, Land Owners and Farmers'. The mill-owners argued that the proposed canal would have to be supplied from springs and rivulets which fed the rivers which drove their mills. They would thus be deprived of their water supply, and the inhabitants would be forced to carry their corn further afield at great inconvenience and expense. They also maintained that since 'good Turnpike Roads' existed for the carriage of coal and lime, the canal and the railway were unnecessary.[5]

In another petition, dated 18 April 1776, the proprietors of the Trent & Mersey Canal argued that the branch should be taken from Cheddleton via Consall to Froghall, and that a 'Rail Way' could be made from there to the limeworks.[6] Giving evidence at the committee stage, Hugh Henshall said that the proposed canal and railway would be 684 chains and 85 links in length from Cheddleton to Froghall. Outside a disputed section of 55 chains, most of the landowners on the route were in agreement with the plan; the owners of 33 chains and 20 links had declared them-selves to be 'neuter'. Permission was given for the new route,[7] and the act (16 Geo III c 32) was finally passed in May 1776.

The tolls were to be 1½d per ton per mile for coal, stone, timber and other goods carried on the canal and railway; and there was to be a special toll of ½d per ton per mile for coal brought from any of the coal-mines in the parishes of Kingsley and Cheadle. The company were authorised to borrow a sum not exceeding £25,000 on the credit of the tolls, and interest on this money was to be paid before any dividends were paid to the proprietors. Edward Leigh, Thomas Mytton and John Beech, who owned coal-mines near Froghall, had agreed to lend £5,000 towards construction costs; until this sum was repaid, with interest at 4½ per cent, half the tolls from coal produced south of the Churnet, were to be vested in the coal-owners. The company made a contract with Thomas Gilbert, John Gilbert, Richard Hill, George Smith, Sampson Whieldon, Henry Copestake, Robert Bill and William Wooliscroft, all owners of limestone quarries, that they would deliver, in the quantities the company required, 'good and merchantable Limestone, ready got and broke, in the Pits where got . . . at the rate of 7d per Ton, each ton to consist of 21 Cwt at 120 lb to the Hundred'. If the owners did not deliver the limestone the company were empowered to enter the quarries and get what they wanted at 2d per ton; and the company agreed to make railways to the face of each limestone pit.

The act mentioned that John Gilbert, Richard Hill, George Smith and Sampson Whieldon were lessees under the Earl of Shrewsbury, who had agreed that the contract would be binding on him and his heirs. The owners of the pits were to agree about the proportions of lime to be supplied, and if they failed to do this, two-fifths were to be supplied by the Earl of Shrewsbury or his lessees out of the quarry in the parish of Alveton (Alton); one-fifth by Thomas Gilbert from the land called the 'Low-pieces'; one-fifth by Henry Copestake from Caldon Low; and the remaining one-fifth by Robert Bill, Sampson Whieldon and William Wooliscroft from the 'Quarter-piece' in the parish of Caldon. The orders were to be for not less than 100 tons, and a deposit of 2d a ton was to be paid. Quantities between 100 and 300 tons were to be delivered after two months, quantities between 300 and 600 tons after three months, and quantities between 600 and 1,000 tons after five months. The following reductions were to be made in the price per ton of lime:

| | Now sold at | | | To be sold at | | | Saving | | |
|---|---|---|---|---|---|---|---|---|---|
| | £ | s | d | £ | s | d | £ | s | d |
| At Shelton | 1 | 0 | 0 | | 10 | 0 | | 10 | 0 |
| At Trentham | 1 | 0 | 0 | | 10 | 10 | | 9 | 2 |
| At Stone | 1 | 0 | 0 | | 11 | 8 | | 8 | 4 |
| At Sandon | 1 | 0 | 0 | | 12 | 6 | | 7 | 6 |
| At Haywood | 1 | 0 | 0 | | 13 | 4 | | 6 | 8 |

The committee of the Trent & Mersey Canal Co met at Stone on 13 June 1776; Thomas Gilbert was chairman and John Sparrow was clerk to the company. The committee considered that the canal and railway would cost about £23,000, in addition to the £5,000 which was to be paid by the colliery owners. The committee resolved to open a subscription for a loan, upon the credit of the tolls, with interest at 4½ per cent; and they decided that the landowners who would benefit by the new concern, and the proprietors of the Grand Trunk, should be given the opportunity to subscribe. It was felt, however, that the proprietors had already made very large contributions through shares and loans, and that some of the proprietors might welcome the chance to transfer from their old securities at the same rate of interest as before.[8]

The branch canal was 17¼ miles long. If left the main line at Etruria top lock in Stoke-on-Trent and followed a 'series of amazing loops and turns'. Originally there were fifteen locks, with eight uphill and seven downhill; the number was later increased to seventeen. The original summit was at Endon, where there was a staircase of two locks. From Cheddleton to Consall, the River Churnet and the canal were parallel; at Oakmeadow Ford lock the canal entered the River Churnet, and for 1½ miles they shared a common course. At Cheddleton there were two water-powered flint-mills, where the machinery had been built by James Brindley; these can still be seen. The Churnet valley, enclosed by wooded hills reaching down to the river and canal, provided an idyllic setting for the carriage of limestone demanded by the iron industry and by agriculture.[9]

According to John Farey, May 1777 saw the opening not only of the Trent & Mersey Canal but also of the branch line to Caldon; and in his contribution to Rees's *Cyclopaedia* (volume VI, 1819) he added that the 'rail-way branch to Mr. Gilbert's Caldon

lime-works' was 'made about the year 1777 or 1778'. As Peter
Lead has pointed out, the canal company was still buying land in
the Shelton area in 1777, and no tolls were collected until 1778.
In March 1778 an agreement was reached regarding the con-
version of the forge at Consall into a flint-mill; and in November
the same year, an agreement was made to build a branch canal,
about ⅝ mile long, from the Caldon branch at Norton to Norton
Green Colliery. This Foxley branch canal had one lock, and
there was a railway from the canal basin to the colliery and the
Ford Green ironworks. From December 1778 until 1791, the
Trent & Mersey Canal Co were buying limestone from Hemingslow Quarry near Caldon Low; this probably means that both
the branch canal and the railway began to operate late in 1778.
Edward Sneyd recorded that the tolls from Christmas 1778 to
Christmas 1779 amounted to £896.[10]

Farey described the railway from Froghall to Caldon Low as
being constructed of cast-iron bars 'spiked down' upon wooden
sleepers; the total was about '20s per yard run'. The line, however,
was 'very crooked, steep, and uneven in its degrees of declivity, in
different parts'.[11] In 1783 the company obtained another act (23
Geo III c 33). They had borrowed £23,660, under the provisions
of an earlier act, but the railway had been found 'to be laid and
placed in a very inconvenient Course and Direction', and had 'not
answered all the good Ends and Purposes thereby intended'. The
new act authorised the extension of the canal 530yd on the level,
and the building of a reservoir at Stanley Moss, later known as
Stanley Pool. The tunnel, which was 76yd long, must have been
constructed under this act, and so must the canal basin, where the
limestone was transhipped into the boats, and large lime-kilns
dominated the scene. The original railway began at Froghall and
ran to Shirley Hollow. It traversed Garston–Foxt lane to Shirley
Common, but it has now disappeared. The second railway went
to Harston Wood, where it turned right to appear above Whiston.
It proceeded past Garston and along Cotton Common to the
limestone quarries. Its length was 3⅛ miles.[12]

In 1783 the amount of money borrowed on the credit of the
tolls of the Caldon Canal was £19,260; in addition, Samuel
Egerton had lent £2,000. Messrs Beech & Co, who owned
collieries near Froghall, had paid £4,848 of their promised
£5,000, and the net profit on the Caldon branch was £2,719.

From 14 June to 27 December 1783 the revenue from tonnage was £13,377, revenue from lime and limestone was £963, and revenue from coal was £34. The charges for the new railway were £2,671, the buildings having cost £250.

Josiah Wedgwood suggested that a 3-mile tunnel might be made from the Caldon branch into the Whitfield coal-mines; the coal-seams could then be worked in the same way as those at Worsley. The route for this tunnel was surveyed and Wedgwood estimated the cost at £1,300 per mile; but nothing came of this idea.

At the General Assembly on 29 March 1785, it was announced that the company had, in the previous two years, spent £6,000 in 'building Warehouses, making Reservoirs for Water, forming and completing a new Railway from the Canal at Froghall to the Limestone Quarries at Caldon, and in other lasting Improvements of the Navigation'. The committee of the Navigation reported to the General Assembly on 25 September 1787 that the Caldon Canal had 'greatly contributed to the assistance' of the main line by carrying waters from its reservoirs to the summit at Harecastle. These reservoirs were Stanley (25ft deep), Knypersley (30ft) and Bagnall (26ft). As the use of lime for agricultural purposes was increasing the success of the branch seemed assured; but in 1790 improvements to the railway at Froghall cost £834, which suggests that the second railway was almost as defective as the first.[13]

In 1802 a railway or tramroad was built, with John Rennie as engineer. The act (42 Geo III c 25) received the royal assent on 15 April, and included provision 'to alter the Course of the Railway from Froghall to Caldon'. The new railway was a double line of flanged plateway, spiked to stone blocks, and five inclined planes were built to effect a total rise of 649ft. According to John Farey, this railway was completed in 1803 and was 'among the most complete works of this kind in Britain'. At Froghall wharf, a store of limestone was held ready for loading into the boats; according to Farey, it was shot into them from ten tippling machines. Short railways led from the tipples to the bottom of the lower Froghall inclined plane which was 65yd long. The loaded wagons were let down singly on one of the railways, and the empty wagons, or those loaded with coal, were drawn up on the other by chains which wound round a large horizontal drum with a regulating brake at the top of the plane. Branch railways were laid from the top of the lower inclined plane to the top of the lime-kilns; from these and from the top of the lower inclined plane a railway about 50yd long led to the bottom of the great Froghall plane, which was about 303yd long. At the top of this plane two wooden pulley wheels turned on vertical axes, and a continuous chain passed round these wheels and similar wheels at the bottom. Five loaded wagons of limestone were hooked to the descending side of the chain, and five empty wagons, or wagons loaded with coal, were hooked to the ascending side. Each wagon carried 22–30cwt of limestone, and their speed was controlled by a brake on one of the pulley wheels.

From the top of the Great Froghall plane the line ran for $\frac{3}{4}$ mile to the bottom of the Whiston plane, which had a similar mechanism of pulley wheels, chain and brake; and from the top of the Whiston plane, it continued for 1 mile to the bottom of Upper Cotton plane. This was 294yd long, and from its top the line ran for $1\frac{3}{4}$ miles to the Caldon Low quarries. The wagons used on this system had projecting pieces of wood hooped with iron at each end to act as shock-absorbers. One horse could draw twelve loaded wagons down the line or twelve empty ones up, but extra horses were needed for coal. The inclined planes were in use from 5.30 am to 5.30 pm, and in that time '18 dozen of Trams of Limestone', or about 270 tons, could be transported. In 1794, on the older railway, one horse had made three journeys on four weekdays, and two on two weekdays, bringing 66cwt of lime down each time, or about 53 tons altogether. The lime company provided the boats and paid the boatmen 9d per ton, which included the cost of the horses and the boys.[14]

The act to authorise an extension of the Caldon branch from Froghall to Uttoxeter was passed on 6 June 1797 (37 Geo III c 81). The tolls were to be $1\frac{1}{2}$d per ton per mile, and John Rennie was appointed engineer. The chief purposes were to carry coal from the Cheadle and Kingsley Moor collieries, to transport copper and brass from Oakamoor and Alton, and to transport lime for agricultural use. The plan was opposed by the Earl of Shrewsbury, who owned the Alton Wire Mill, and by the Cheadle Brass Co, which leased the mill from the Earl; their objection was that the canal would restrict the water supply to the mill. The original plan was deposited at Stafford on 23 September 1801. It proposed that the canal should flow into the millpond and out again before

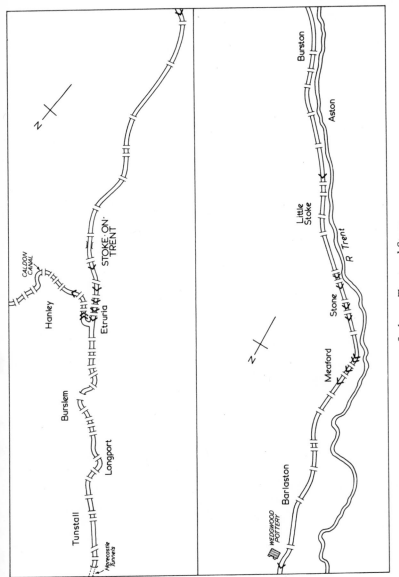

4 Stoke-on-Trent and Stone

reaching the wire-mill, and that it should continue at the same level through Abbey Wood until it reached Slain Hollow.

The construction of this canal was delayed, and at one time it seemed as if the project was going to be abandoned. On 31 May 1800 the *Staffordshire Advertiser* invited contractors to apply for 'the forming and starting the ground for a Railway from Froghall to the Turnpike Road on Stub-wood, and from the said Road to Spath near Uttoxeter, in two distinct lots, to a Plan and Specification now laying at the Canal Office in Stone'. Two years later, however, the idea of a canal was in favour again, and in 1802 an act (42 Geo III c 25) was passed which authorised a variation of the proposed course near Alveton or Alton Mill.

On 15 July 1802 the *Derby Mercury* advertised for contractors for the construction of a canal from Froghall to Uttoxeter; tenders were to be delivered to 'Mr. Robinson at the Navigation Office, Stone'. Work was delayed until about 1805. On 25 April 1806 the Cheadle Brass Co instructed Matthew Brindley, a relative of the great engineer, 'to pursue the line of the canal from Froghall to Alton Mills to examine whether the Navigation Company make use of, or divert any stream or streams of water belonging to the R. Churnet, and to make reports accordingly'. He appears to have ignored this instruction, for the company resolved 'that Mr. Matthew Brindley be referred to an order made by the Co ... respecting his pursuing from time to time the line of the Canal from Froghall to Oakamoor ... which order does not seem yet to have been complied with'.

On 26 February 1808 the Company of the Proprietors of the Navigation from the Trent to the Mersey presented another petition, in which they stated that the authorised branch canals and railways had been completed, except for the branch to Uttoxeter. The canal reached Oakamoor in August of that year and early in 1809 it had almost reached Alton. On 13 March 1809 an agreement was reached between the canal proprietors and the Alton Wire Mill; this was signed by the Earl of Shrewsbury, who was a shareholder in the latter concern. This agreement permitted the canal to pass through part of the millpond; in return the canal company agreed to construct a new weir and pond for the mill, 18in above the level of the original pond. An act of 20 May 1809 (49 Geo III c 73) authorised a loan of £30,000 to enable the canal company to complete the canal. On

3 September 1811 it was officially opened.

On 20 September 1811 *The Times* reported that the news of the opening had been received in Uttoxeter 'with great demonstration of joy by the inhabitants of that town and neighbourhood'. On 14 September 1811 the *Staffordshire Advertiser* gave a full account of the rejoicing at Uttoxeter:

> In the extensive basin lay two elegant pleasure boats for the use of the proprietors and their friends ... with four or five other boats ... The *Prince Regent* boat took the lead and proceeded in good style to the beautiful cast-iron aqueduct over the River Tean ... After passing Rocester, where upwards of 300 persons belonging to Mr. Briddon's cotton works attended ... the boats arrived at two o'clock in the grand weir across the River Churnet at Crump Wood.

About 150 people were invited to a 'cold collation', and after speeches, toasts and songs, the guests returned to Uttoxeter about 5pm. The poor of Uttoxeter were entertained with bonfires and were given free bread and a share of two roasted sheep.

The canal had seventeen locks from Froghall to Uttoxeter, and was 13¼ miles long. At Alton there was a tunnel 40yd long, and the River Churnet was crossed on the level, with controlling locks on each side. The River Tean was crossed by an iron aqueduct, while a tramroad, the Woodhead Plateway, ran from collieries at Woodhead Hall, Cheadle, to a wharf near Jackson's Wood; at this wharf there was a large basin, where coal was loaded into the boats. The next lock was officially called Morris's lock, but was known locally as California lock. At Uttoxeter there were several large warehouses. In 1818 it was claimed that the canal had contributed to the prosperity of the market-town, which was renowned for its cattle, sheep, butter, cheese, corn and other provisions. Plans for a branch from Rocester to Ashbourne were considered in 1813, and plans for a branch from Uttoxeter to Ashbourne and Little Eaton in 1824. These projects, and the plan of 1839 for a canal from Uttoxeter to Burton-on-Trent, came to nothing.[15]

In 1796 the Trent & Mersey Co attempted to promote a bill for making a branch from the Caldon Canal at Endon to Leek, together with a feeder from a reservoir at Rudyard Lake near Leek. The reservoir was urgently needed, as the main line often had to be supplied from the Caldon branch in times of drought. There was considerable opposition to the bill, particularly from the inhabitants of Chester and from those who lived near the line of the Chester Canal. Opponents of the bill suspected that the company's real purpose was to 'lay hold of all the Supplies of Water in the Country, with the View to prevent the Possibility of any Communication being formed with the Chester Canal'. It was claimed that the Chester Canal, 'for Want of a Communication with other Canals', was 'useless to the Public', and that 'the Benefits which would otherwise arise to the agricultural and commercial Interests of the County of Chester and Town of Nantwich, and their Neighbourhood' were thus 'entirely withheld'.[16]

The bill was held up by this opposition and, for a time, consideration was given to an alternative plan drawn up by Benjamin Outram. This plan involved the construction of a canal from the Peak Forest Canal near Marple via Macclesfield and Rudyard to the Caldon branch about 4 miles from Leek; it included a reservoir at Rudyard.[17] On 22 March 1797, however, the Lords approved the original scheme. The act (37 Geo III c 36) was entitled 'An Act to enable the Company of Proprietors of the Navigation from the Trent to the Mersey to make a navigable canal from and out of a certain Branch of their said Navigation, called the Caldon Canal, at or near Endon, to or near Leek in Staffordshire, and also a Reservoir for supplying the several canals of the said Company with water'. In order to placate the Grand Junction Canal, which was a broad canal, the Trent & Mersey Co agreed to a clause which required them to widen their canal after a certain time; but this was never done.

The construction of the branch to Leek, which was $2\frac{3}{4}$ miles long, involved an alteration in the summit of the Caldon branch. This summit was originally between the top of Stockton locks and Endon (Park Lane), where there was a staircase pair of locks from which the canal continued level to Cheddleton. The locks at Endon were removed, and the summit was extended to Hazelhurst by means of a new course above the old one. A set of three staircase locks was built at Hazelhurst to lead the canal back into the original course. The Leek branch proceeded from the town, passed through a tunnel 130yd long and after following the valley joined the new line above the locks at Hazelhurst. The original course from Endon to Hazelhurst was abandoned. The

Plate 1    Preston Brook: the junction of the Trent & Mersey and Bridge-
          water Canals (*Airviews Ltd Manchester Airport*)

Plate 2    Preston Brook: the south entrance to Preston Brook tunnel (*Harry
          Arnold*)

*Plate 3* The Anderton lift from the River Weaver *(Harry Arnold)*

*Plate 4* An aerial view of the Anderton lift *(Airviews Ltd Manchester Airport)*

Leek branch was declared complete in an act of 1802 (42 Geo III c 25). It supplied the town with cheap coal and provided better communication with markets, thus fulfilling in some measure the hope, expressed on 3 November 1793, that 'the Capital of the moorlands' might 'become a Port'. In 1841–2 the three-lock staircase which had proved unsatisfactory was replaced by three separate locks at Hollinhurst. The original line was reopened between Hollinhurst and Denford in order to form a link with the main route to Froghall. This necessitated the building of an aqueduct at Hazelhurst, where the reopened line to Froghall had to pass under the Leek branch.[18]

There were many plans for a canal to Macclesfield. In 1765–6 there was a plan for a canal from Witton Bridge via Knutsford, Macclesfield and Stockport to Manchester, and in 1793 there was a proposal that the Caldon branch should be extended to Macclesfield via Leek. In 1793 the Peak Forest Canal was promoted by Samuel Oldknow, the first manufacturer of British muslin, who owned spinning mills at Stockport, at Mellor and at Marple. Oldknow also owned estates at Mellor and Marple, and was a well-known agricultural improver.

One of the main objects of the Peak Forest Canal was to bring limestone, both for building and for agricultural purposes, from the deposits at Doveholes, south-east of Whaley Bridge. On 5 December 1793 the canal committee met the agent of the Duke of Devonshire at Disley and sought his consent for the proposed canal. The act was passed during the canal boom on 28 March 1794, and the canal was opened on 1 May 1800, except for the locks at Marple, which were completed in 1804. There was an aqueduct at Marple which was considered a great engineering feat and was known locally as the 'Grand Aqueduct'. Oldknow originally held fifty-two shares in the Peak Forest Canal Co, and he owned lime-kilns near the canal at Marple, which began working in 1797. The canal terminated at Bugsworth, and a 6½-mile tramroad linked it with the quarries. It had a connection through the Ashton Canal at Dukinfield Junction with the Rochdale Canal at Manchester; as this canal joined the Calder & Hebble Navigation, which linked with the Aire & Calder Canal, there was also a connection with Yorkshire. Through the Ashton, Rochdale and Bridgewater Canals there was also a link with the Trent & Mersey; and during the construction of the Peak Forest Canal, the advantage of connecting the top level with the Trent & Mersey was discussed. John Nuttall surveyed a line for a canal from the summit level of the Caldon branch at Endon to the top level of the Peak Forest Canal at Marple. This survey was revised by Benjamin Outram and printed on 10 March 1796; but the scheme was rejected by the Lords, having been opposed by the Duke of Bridgewater and by rival canal companies. Its opponents included the Trent & Mersey Co, which saw a threat to its own plan for a branch from the Caldon branch to Leek.[19]

A branch canal or railway from Marple to the Poynton and Norbury collieries was proposed unsuccessfully by the Peak Forest Co in 1799; and in 1805 and 1806 there was an attempt to get the Trent & Mersey Co to support a projected line from Macclesfield to near Lawton. This, too, failed, as did similar proposals made in 1810 and between 1814 and 1818.

On 6 October 1824 a successful meeting was held in Macclesfield to promote a canal linking the Peak Forest with the Trent & Mersey, and £60,000 was subscribed for this purpose. The incentive for the scheme at this date was the promotion of the Cromford & High Peak Railway, which was authorised in May 1825. The engineer for the railway was Josiah Jessop, son of William. The route began at Cromford, rose 990ft by inclines to a summit of 1,264ft, and descended 747ft to a connection with the Peak Forest Canal at Whaley Bridge. This connection would have diverted traffic from the Trent & Mersey, so the company supported the plan for a canal to Macclesfield with links to the Trent & Mersey via the Hall Green branch. Thomas Telford surveyed the line linking the Peak Forest Canal and the Trent & Mersey Canal. It was 26 miles long from Marple, the junction with the Peak Forest Canal, to Hardings Wood, the junction with the Trent & Mersey. Telford did not build the canal, as he left to construct the Birmingham & Liverpool Junction Canal, but he gave advice on the Hall Green branch, since he was then engaged on the Harecastle tunnel. The Macclesfield Canal followed a straight course, which made huge cuttings and embankments necessary; this was typical of Telford's works. There was a flight of twelve locks at Bosley to reach the 518ft summit level; and there was a stop-lock at Hall Green, where a 1ft rise prevented loss of water from the Trent & Mersey. The engineer was William Crosley, and the canal was opened in 1831, the same year as the Cromford & High Peak

Railway. It faced great competition from the Trent & Mersey Canal and the Cromford & High Peak Railway, but it proved useful as a means of transporting cotton and coal from the mills and mines established near its course.

James Potter was the resident engineer of the Trent & Mersey when the Hall Green branch was being built, and on 19 October 1827 he reported that the work had begun. The contractors were Daniel Pritchard and William Hoof, who were also the contractors for the new tunnel at Harecastle. On 20 March 1829 Telford made a report to James Caldwell, the chairman of the canal company, on 'that portion of the Macclesfield Canal now executing at the Expense of the Company'. He had found that it was 'generally going on properly'; but he reported that he had had 'occasion to object to the use of blue Clunch with which it was intended to cover the lining, instead of with Gravel'. This type of clunch, 'although hard when taken from its natural bed', was 'sure to be dissolved into a soft pulp when exposed to Water'. He had therefore given orders 'that none should be used, that now laid down removed, and a Coating of Gravel laid on the Puddle'.

Telford also reported that there was water in the banks to the east of the embankment, and that the source of this water was above the level of the canal. This was dangerous, because the water might get behind the lining and cause damage. There was a proposal to 'pave the Canal with flat stones below the clay lining in order to prevent the back water or sand from rising'; but as this was an 'uncertain and expensive operation', Telford recommended that the water be intercepted 'by means of Drains' and thus brought into the canal 'at a proper level'.

On 6 May 1829 William Faram of Lawton reported to Telford that they had begun 'bottom-cutting' at Hall Green, and had found a great quantity of water in the sand, which they could not remove by drains. As this meant that the puddle or lining would not stay in place, they had 'sheeted about 7yd forward with Stone at the place the water built up worst'. They found that the stone stayed in its place, and that the water issued 'between the points of the Stone', bringing very little sand with it. Faram considered it necessary 'to face the sides of the Canal with stone on part'. He explained that the water was 'in the sand near the whole depth of the Canal', and added: 'I am afraid the Puddle will not stand.'

The Hall Green branch was 1½ miles long; it left the Trent & Mersey Canal at Hardings Wood and joined the Macclesfield Canal at Hall Green. On this branch the tolls were slightly higher than on the Trent & Mersey, but the same as on the Macclesfield. If the water level was lower in the branch than in the Macclesfield, the boats of the Macclesfield were not allowed to pass the stop-lock at Hall Green without the permission of the Trent & Mersey Co.[20]

In November 1826 James Caldwell reported that the Ellesmere & Chester Canal Co had given notice of their intention to apply to Parliament for authority to make a canal from Wardle in Cheshire to communicate with and 'be cut into' the Trent & Mersey Canal 'in the Township of Middlewich'. Caldwell argued that this communication would be 'very prejudicial' to the Trent & Mersey, and that it would be a direct violation of the Chester Canal act (17 Geo III c 67), under which the Chester Co were debarred from 'making, carrying on, or extending' their canal 'nearer in any part to the navigable Canal from the Trent to the Mersey than One Hundred Yards'. Under that protection, the Trent & Mersey Co had confidently expended a 'vast Capital' in making their canal 'beneficial and convenient to the Trade and Commerce of the Kingdom, and in particular to that of Liverpool, Manchester, Birmingham, and London, for which it is amply sufficient', and they were now engaged in making an additional tunnel and an additional reservoir, for which they had been obliged to borrow £50,000 at interest on the security of the tolls. Caldwell urged the proprietors of the Trent & Mersey to fight the bill.

Unfortunately, the Trent & Mersey was already faced with competition from the Birmingham & Liverpool Junction Canal. This canal, which obtained its act in 1826, connected with the Chester Canal at Nantwich and with the Staffordshire & Worcestershire Canal at Autherley; it thus gave a shorter route from Birmingham to Liverpool than the Trent & Mersey. The proprietors, therefore, decided not to fight the Ellesmere & Chester Canal Co but to join them, and they did this by obtaining an act (7 & 8 Geo IV c 102), which authorised them to build a very short Wardle Green branch linking the Trent & Mersey with the Ellesmere & Chester's proposed Middlewich branch.

The Wardle Green section was built by the Trent & Mersey Co, and was only 110yd long. The bridge over the entrance was inscribed 'Wardle Canal 1829', and the Ellesmere & Chester's Middlewich branch began at the head of the Wardle lock. The Wardle Green section of the Trent & Mersey was opened on 1 September 1833. The company levied tolls on it of 9d per ton on coal, culm, coke, limestone and rock salt; 9½d per ton on freestone, timber, ironstone, slate, lead-ore, iron and lead; and 10½d per ton on all other goods. These high tolls discouraged trade between Manchester and Birmingham, but were justified by the company on the ground that the proprietors wished to prevent the Ellesmere & Chester Canal from taking away the Trent & Mersey's through traffic.[21] The tolls were intended, in fact, to prevent the Trent & Mersey traffic from proceeding to Liverpool by the Ellesmere & Chester.

In 1798 there was a plan for a canal from the lime works at Lilleshall to the Trent & Mersey 'at or near Stone', with a branch to Market Drayton. This scheme was intended to connect the Trent & Mersey with the Donnington Wood Canal, which was made up of small canals linking Shrewsbury, Donnington Wood, Pave Lane, Ketley, Coalport and Coalbrookdale. It was never carried out.[22]

An act of 6 June 1797 (37 Geo III c 81) authorised short branch canals in the Potteries from Shelton to Cobridge, from Longport to Dale Hall in Burslem, and from Sideway House near Stoke-on-Trent to Lane End. The tolls were to be 1½d per ton per mile, and the expense of construction was to be borne by the Trent & Mersey Canal Co. The Burslem branch was completed in 1805, but an act of 15 April 1802 (42 Geo III c 25) authorised railways from the Trent & Mersey Canal to Lane End, Hanley and Burslem; it was said that these would be 'of great Advantage to the extensive Manufactories established at these Places'. In 1816 it was reported that the railway from Stoke to Lane End in Longton was carrying wagons which took materials and packages to the neighbourhood of Lane Delph and Lane End and returned with crates.

The length of this railway was 2⅝ furlongs, and near Longton station it divided into two short branches: one went down Market Street and the other along Edensor Road. The railway from Hanley started from the market-place, and its wagons brought packages into the town and returned with crates and casks of porcelain and pottery. It terminated in Vale Pleasant near Etruria, and was 6¾ furlongs long, with a branch to the junction of Sun Street and Broad Street. The railway from Dale Hall to Burslem went from near the terminus of the Burslem branch canal to near St John's Square, a distance of 5¾ furlongs.[23]

In its original form the Trent & Mersey Canal did not connect with the Trent Navigation at Burton, as it passed about a mile west of the town and ran parallel to the River Trent to Wilden Ferry. The Trent had been navigable for boats and barges from Wilden Ferry to Burton from 1699; under the act of that year William Lord Paget was authorised to charge the fixed rate of 3d per ton per mile upon all goods conveyed by the navigation. Lord Paget leased the navigation to the Burton Boat Co, and near the Fleetstones in Bond End, beyond which the powers of the act did not extend, they constructed a basin with wharfs and a stone causeway. About 1774–5 the lessees of the Trent Navigation made the Bond End Canal across the private property of Lord Paget's descendant, the Earl of Uxbridge. This canal, which was made without an act, had a basin about 40yd from the Trent & Mersey Canal at Shobnall, and it was included in a renewed lease to the Burton Boat Co in 1784. In September 1787 Thomas Sparrow, the clerk to the Trent & Mersey Co, reported that the committee had held a conference with the proprietors of the 'Burton Navigation' about a proposed connection, but that the terms proposed were unacceptable. In September 1790, however, it was reported to the General Assembly that an attempt had been made to obtain by 'Violence and Force' what 'could not be accomplished by legal Proceedings'. The reference is obviously to the ground between the Bond End Canal and the Trent & Mersey at Shobnall:

> A set of Men protected by an armed Multitude, have lately cut through the Towing Path and Banks of this Canal, for the Purpose of opening a Passage for Boats into another Navigation, parallel in its Course to a Part of this – The Committee have, however, obtained the most able Advice on the Occasion, and have directed such Steps to be taken as they doubt not will bring to Justice the Proprietors of this Outrage.

The rule of law prevailed, and the cut was filled in.

The Burton Boat Co, however, adopted other methods to bring

pressure on the Trent & Mersey Co. In particular, they supported schemes which would have bypassed the Trent & Mersey between Burton-on-Trent and Fradley Junction. After a meeting at the Grand Junction Canal's offices in December 1793, the Trent & Mersey Canal Co decided that they would build the Shobnall link, and a plan was prepared on 13 September 1794. This plan showed a small basin and one lock, and gave the fall as 3ft 9in. On 6 February 1795 the Trent & Mersey Canal Co presented a petition concerning a link between the Bond End and the Trent & Mersey at Shobnall, which would 'open an easy Commercial Intercourse between the two canals'. Thomas Sparrow gave evidence and leave was given to bring in a bill for this canal. Petitions against the scheme were heard on 9 April 1795 from Francis, Earl of Moira, who claimed that it would be injurious to his property; from the Earl of Uxbridge and his lessees; from the owners and occupiers of mills, forges and other works upon the River Trent between Wychnor and Cavendish Bridge, who were against the bill because it would divert water from the river; and from the owners of fisheries between those places. On 22 April 1795 there was a further petition against the scheme from Thomas, Duke of Newcastle. Despite this opposition the bill was passed; it gained the royal assent on 2 June 1795. The Shobnall cut had one lock and a stop-lock, and was 1⅛ miles long.

For Burton, the construction of the Trent & Mersey Canal had opened an additional connection with Liverpool, Manchester and Birmingham, and in 1791 Burton was a flourishing town with nine 'common brewers'. The breweries included that of Michael Bass and that of William Worthington & Sons. The oak for the casks came from the Baltic, the iron hoops from south Staffordshire. Brewing became the main trade of Burton and increasing quantities of beer were sent to London, Birmingham, Liverpool, Manchester and other towns with which there was a canal connection. The traffic to Gainsborough and Hull for the export of ale to St Petersburg was checked in 1822, when Russia imposed a high import duty on all English ales.[24]

# 4

# The Years of Success

The opening of the Trent & Mersey Canal gave a powerful stimulus to the development of the Potteries. Coal and clay were to be found throughout the area: coal was mined at Lane End, Ubberley, Bucknall, Shelton, Norton Biddulph and Burslem. The crate-makers were kept busy producing the crates in which the pottery was packed. The demand for grain and flour increased, and the canal made it possible to bring supplies from the Baltic. The advantages of canal transport were highlighted in 1800, when grain was scarce and prices were as high as 127s a quarter. The committee of the Trent & Mersey Canal decided to forgo tolls on wheat for two months and tried to prevent merchants from pushing up the prices artificially:

> The Committee appointed for managing the affairs of this Navigation, desirous of contributing their endeavours to relieve the distress of the Poor and labouring parts of the Community by giving encouragement to a seasonable Importation of Corn, have Resolved and Agreed, that all Wheat imported and brought upon this Navigation after the 25th instant shall be permitted to pass FREE of TONNAGE, and all other dues, for the space of Two Months from the said 25th instant.
>
> AND for the purpose of preventing every tendency to Monopoly and other unlawful practices . . . the Company have expressly ORDERED and directed, that no Corn shall be received into any of the Warehouses of the Company, unless accompanied with a regular Consignment, or shall remain therein for a longer space of time than may be necessary for providing vessels to convey it to its place of destination.
>
> Thomas Sparrow,
> Stone, 23 October, 1800. Clerk to the Company.

An editorial in the *Derby Mercury* commented: 'The Utility of the Canals was never more conspicuous than at the present period. For some months past the neighbouring counties have been principally fed by wheat brought by water from Liverpool, Hull, etc.'[1]

The completion of the Staffordshire & Worcestershire Canal in 1772 established a connection from the Trent & Mersey to the Severn; in September 1772 the Staffordshire & Worcestershire was linked with the Birmingham Canal. The establishment of a connection with the Thames was more complicated; the canal from Fradley to Oxford was not completed until 1790.

Josiah Wedgwood was very much in favour of connections with the Coventry and Oxford Canals, but, as Charles Hadfield has shown in *The Canals of the East Midlands* (David & Charles, 1966), the progress of these canals was delayed by disputes about where they should meet. The real issue was tolls: the Coventry Canal Co could take tolls on coal for the first 2 miles of the Oxford Canal from the junction, and the Oxford Canal could take tolls on all articles except coal which were carried for up to $3\frac{1}{2}$ miles on the Coventry Canal in the direction of Coventry. The Oxford Canal tried to change the junction from Longford to Bedworth, which had originally been suggested; this would have meant that coal from the Bedworth Colliery would not pay tolls on the Coventry Canal. The result was that for a time the two canals were parallel and very close to each other for more than a mile before the junction was reached.

The Trent & Mersey Co promoted a bill which would have forced the Coventry Co to complete their canal, but this was defeated. The scheme for a junction between the Birmingham Canal and the Coventry Canal at Fazeley was more successful. On 20 June 1782 at a meeting at Coleshill between representatives of the Oxford, Coventry and Trent & Mersey Canal Companies, it was decided that the Oxford Co would finish building their canal to Oxford, and that the Coventry Co would build theirs to Fazeley by raising £30,000 through the issue of an additional 750 shares of £40 each. These shares were never issued, and eventually £40,000 had to be borrowed on the security of the tolls. The Birmingham & Fazeley Canal, once it had obtained its act, was to build $5\frac{1}{2}$ miles of the Coventry Canal Co's line to Whittington Brook. The $5\frac{1}{2}$ miles from Whittington Brook to Fradley was to be built by the Trent & Mersey Canal Co. The Coventry Canal Co would be able to buy back the Trent & Mersey's section within two months of completion, at a cost which would include interest.

In 1784 the Birmingham Canal Co amalgamated with the Birmingham & Fazeley Canal Co, and the new amalgamated concern started to build the line to Fazeley. The Coventry Canal extension from Athelstone to Fazeley was then surveyed by Robert Whitworth, and Thomas Dadford senior gave advice on the proposed aqueduct over the Tame. In 1785, however, the Coventry Canal Co attempted to sabotage this line by promoting a scheme to make the rivers Tame and Anker navigable to Atherstone; the coal-owners around Atherstone welcomed this, as they did not want coal brought by the Birmingham & Fazeley to compete with theirs. Despite this opposition, the act (25 Geo III c 99) to authorise the agreement at Coleshill was passed. On 29 March 1785 Thomas Sparrow reported that the committee of the Trent & Mersey were 'fully persuaded that the Completion of the Coventry Canal from . . . Fradley Heath to Atherstone' would 'greatly increase the Utility' of their own navigation. The committee had therefore 'ordered the most vigorous and effectual Measures to be taken in Parliament for accomplishing this End'; and they urged the proprietors 'to exert their mutual endeavours for obtaining it'.

At the request of the Trent & Mersey Canal Co, the Court of King's Bench gave a ruling upholding the decisions already made, and in June 1785 the Coventry Co agreed to build the line to Fazeley, employing Thomas Sheasby senior as engineer. The Coventry and Oxford Canals agreed in the same year to have their junction at Hawkesbury instead of Longford; this made almost all the parallel cuts unnecessary, but as the Oxford Canal was nearly 7in higher than the Coventry, a stop-lock was needed. The Trent & Mersey's line from Fradley to Whittington Brook was built under the direction of Thomas Dadford senior. On 26 September 1786 the proprietors of the Trent & Mersey were informed that the Oxford Co were finishing the remainder of their undertaking, that the Coventry Co had contracted with engineers to finish the remainder of their canal, and that the Trent & Mersey Co had finished the 'greatest part' of the canal between Fradley Heath and Fazeley; there was therefore a 'certain prospect of these several Works being brought to a conclusion'. On 25 September 1787 Thomas Sparrow reported that the 'Fazeley Canal' had not been completed because of the 'negligence of the undertaker'; some parts of the towpath and fences were still to be finished. The canal was 'wholly cut', however, and he expected it to be ready in a month.

On 30 September 1788 the committee of the Trent & Mersey reported that the canal from Fradley Heath to Fazeley had been finished for 'some Time'. As the act had stipulated, the Coventry Co purchased the section built by the Trent & Mersey for £10,541 (cost plus interest). The original estimate for the canal from Fradley Heath to Fazeley had been £13,854. This had been for a canal 26ft wide at the surface with a depth of 4ft 6in, and had included six road-bridges and seven other bridges, together with 65 acres of land for the canal and towpath at £40 an acre. On 29 September 1789 it was reported that the canals from Fazeley to Birmingham and from Coventry to Oxford had been completed. The canal from Fazeley to the Coventry was also complete, except that the aqueduct over the River Tame had been delayed by floods. The proprietors of these canals had 'already experienced very considerable Benefits from their several Works'. They had previously resented the action taken by the Trent & Mersey to make them 'finish their Undertakings', but they were now beginning to regard the company as their 'Friends and Benefactors'. On 13 July 1790, the Tame aqueduct having been completed, the canal from Atherstone to Fazeley was opened.[2]

After 1790 the Trent & Mersey had to fight hard for several years to expand trade and preserve its competitive position. On 28 September 1790 the committee reported the growing prosperity of the canal, but warned: 'The Spirit of Speculation and Enterprize which the Works of Inland Navigation, and especially those early formed, have excited, give constant occasion for vigilance and Circumspection, to prevent Innovations on the properties of the first Adventurers, by new Projects yearly offered to Parliament.' At the same time, they offered some reassurance: 'The Grand Trunk, happy in its Patrons and Protectors, has hitherto withstood every Attack, founded on Pretensions to superior Merit, or Parliamentary Favour.'[3]

In 1793, in an effort to expand trade, the Trent & Mersey Co tried to promote a canal to be called the Trent Canal, which would run from the Trent at Derwent Mouth across the Erewash Canal to the Trent at Nottingham. A subscription list was opened with sums of £400 each from John Sparrow and Josiah Wedgwood, and the proposal was backed by the Erewash Canal Co. It was opposed, however, by the Trent Navigation Co, and in May 1793 an agreement was reached that the proposal would be withdrawn on condition that a thorough survey of the river should be made as a preliminary to legislation by the navigation company to obtain improvements.

The plans for the Trent Canal had involved a branch from Derby to the Trent & Mersey at Shardlow, but this was abandoned with the rest of the scheme. Authority was obtained, however, for an independent Derby Canal from Derby to the Trent & Mersey at Swarkestone with extensions to Denby and Sandiacre and a branch to Little Eaton. The act (33 Geo III c 102) was passed on 7 May 1793 and the engineer was Benjamin Outram. The canal, whose dividends were limited to 8 per cent, was completed on 30 June 1796. Between Swarkestone and the River Trent there was a 3-furlong link with four locks, and a compensation toll of 1s had to be paid to the Trent & Mersey Canal Co on all goods passing along this connection. This connection was a commercial failure; in 1812 the cost of maintenance exceeded the revenue, and by 1837 it had been drained. The Derby Canal made Derby an important inland port, and brought considerable trade to the Trent & Mersey. Ironstone and iron were brought to Swarkestone, and goods from Cheshire and the Potteries came to Swarkestone, Derby and Langley Mill.[4]

On 13 April 1775 the royal assent had been given to an act (15 Geo III c 16) to enable Sir Nigel Gresley and his son Nigel Bowyer Gresley to make a canal from their coal-mines in Apedale to Newcastle-under-Lyme. The act authorised them to make the canal at their own expense, and controlled the price of coal in Newcastle-under-Lyme for forty-two years. The canal, 3 miles long, went from the collieries at Apedale to a basin on Liverpool Road, which led into Newcastle-under-Lyme. Originally, a branch to Newcastle-under-Lyme had been envisaged as part of the general plan of the Trent & Mersey Canal project, but the idea was not revived until early in 1795, partly because Sir Nigel Gresley's Canal had acquired control of the coal trade in the town. On 5 February 1795, a petition of the 'Gentlemen, Clergy, Free-

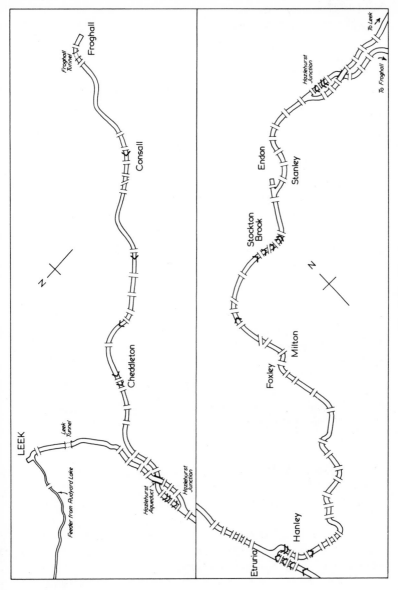

5 The Caldon Canal

holders, Traders, and other Inhabitants of the County of Stafford' was presented to the Commons. This said that surveys had been taken, and that it seemed practicable to make a canal from Stoke-on-Trent to Newcastle-under-Lyme 'for the Navigation of Boats and other Vessels with heavy Burthens'. Such a canal, it was claimed, would 'facilitate the Carriage and Conveyance of Lime, Limestone, Iron and other Merchandize', and 'tend greatly to the Improvement of the adjacent Lands, the Ease and Convenience of the Manufactories and the Preservation of the Public Utility'.

The bill had its first reading on 17 February 1795, but on 18 March the inhabitants of Stoke petitioned against the plan. The proposed line would cross the River Trent below Stoke, and this made the petitioners fear that in times of flooding the river would be impounded and many of the houses flooded. They proposed a new line leading from a piece of land belonging to the trustees of George Boughey through the 'Village of Stoke' into the Trent & Mersey in another piece of land called Quinton's Wood. This deviation was accepted; and despite petitions from Sir Nigel Bowyer Gresley and the Earl of Uxbridge, who claimed that the canal would injure their property, the act (25 Geo III c 87) was given the royal assent on 2 June 1795. Until the forty-two years had expired, no coal was to be carried on the canal to places mentioned in Gresley's act; but an exception was made for coal selling at less than 8s a ton and used in the manufacture of pottery.[5] The canal left the main line at Stoke, proceeded southwards, turned west after reaching the ridge between Stoke and Newcastle-under-Lyme, and finally ran north to its terminus at the southern end of Brook Lane.

Newcastle-under-Lyme was a market town and had grown up in the twelfth century around a castle. It gained its importance from its site on a main route linking London and Birmingham, which crossed into Cheshire at Lawton. Even after the opening of the Trent & Mersey Canal, Newcastle remained a coaching centre. In 1797 the borough council approved a plan for the construction of a Junction Canal from the 'Newcastle or Lower Canal to pass through the Stubbs, the Marsh, and the Brampton to join Sir Nigel Gresley's canal near the house called the Gate'. In 1798 an act (38 Geo III c 29) was passed which authorised, in addition to the canal, a railway ½ mile long from Gresley's canal at Apedale to the coal and other works at Partridge Nest and Bignall End, and a railway ¼ mile long to connect with the canal at Stubbs Walk and with the Newcastle-under-Lyme Canal near its basin.

The authorised capital was £80,000 in £50 shares; and as long as the limitation on Gresley's price for coal was enforced, the transport of coal was prohibited. The canal, which was 1⅛ miles long, was soon completed, but no railways were built. The plan for an inclined plane to link the two canals has been a subject of local controversy for some time, but Peter Lead and Charles Hadfield have demonstrated conclusively on the basis of field evidence and documentary evidence provided by the minute books of the Newcastle-under-Lyme Junction Canal Co (1825–63), that this inclined plane was never built. The incline, which would have been about 70ft long, would have had to cross the Tittensor–Talke turnpike road, and this would have necessitated earthworks and embankments in Brook Lane; no evidence of such works survives. The fact that the connection was not made resulted in the traffic being very limited; but the wharf at Marsh received coal, as it was more convenient than the terminus of Gresley's canal. Because it carried no through traffic, the Newcastle-under-Lyme Canal was not a success; its first dividend was not paid until 1840 and amounted to only £1 a share.[6] Unlike Stoke, Newcastle-under-Lyme did not benefit much from inland navigation.

Sir Nigel Gresley was one of the promoters of the Commercial Canal, which was projected in 1795. This plan was motivated by the desire to have a wide canal from London to the Mersey, and was an attempt to force the Trent & Mersey, Coventry and Oxford Canals to widen parts of their existing routes. The scheme was for a canal from Nantwich via Uttoxeter to the Ashby Canal. The line was surveyed first by Robert Whitworth and then by William Jessop. It led from Nantwich to a junction with Sir Nigel's canal or the Newcastle-under-Lyme Junction Canal, crossed first the Trent & Mersey and then the Caldon branch, passed via the Dilhorne and Cheadle coalfield to Uttoxeter, joined the Trent & Mersey below Horninglow (Burton), and finally crossed the River Trent to link up with the Ashby Canal. The scheme was opposed by the Trent & Mersey Co, but was supported by the 'manufacturers of earthenware in the Potteries',

who set up a committee of subscribers. It was also supported by
the Burton Navigation, and by some of the proprietors of the
Ashby and Chester Canals. The act of 1797 which authorised an
extension of the Trent & Mersey from Froghall to Uttoxeter was
obtained largely for the purpose of defeating the proposed Commercial Canal, and the delay in building the Uttoxeter extension
was partly due to a lack of enthusiasm for the scheme once the
Commercial Canal project had been defeated. This defeat was
brought about by a promise from the Trent & Mersey Canal Co,
written into the act for the Leek branch and reservoir in 1796,
that if the Grand Junction Canal were finished from Braunston
to Brentford, and if the Oxford and Coventry Canals would widen
their sections from Braunston, they would widen their canal from
Fradley to Harecastle within two years. This agreement meant
that the Grand Junction Canal dropped its support for the 'Great
Commercial Canal', and after 1797 the project was given up.
Having successfully overcome a serious attempt to bypass their
route, the Trent & Mersey did not widen their canal.[7]

The success of the Trent & Mersey owed much to its control of
routes from Liverpool and Manchester via the Potteries to Hull
and London; but some credit should be given to the efficient
organisation of the canal, especially in its early years. Volume I
of Wedgwood's *Commonplace Book* gives details of proposals for
the 'better regulation of our canal boats and new captains'. These
included the numbering and gauging of the boats, and the issue
of waybills to the captains, so that entries could be made by the
wharfingers, surveyors and captains concerning cargoes and
locations. Josiah Wedgwood recommended that these waybills
should be examined by an auditor, whose analysis would identify
'proper objects ... for praise or reward, for censure and for
punishment'. Wedgwood added that if this were not done there
would be 'an end of all emulation to meet the good opinions of
their employers'. If it was done, Wedgwood believed the employees would be 'doubly careful of their cargoes, – of the banks, –
the locks – or whatever they have to do with'. These waybills for
each boat were to be bound in a separate volume, so that the
complete collection would provide a 'history of all the business
done by our boats'. Wedgwood anticipated criticisms that this
procedure would be too time-consuming by pointing out that
'the single article of conveyance of goods' was the ultimate object

Plate 5    The Harecastle tunnel: the north end *(Harry Arnold)*

Plate 6    The Harecastle tunnel: the south end *(Harry Arnold)*

Plate 7    The Caldon branch at Hanley *(Waterways News, British Waterways Board)*

Plate 8    The Hazelhurst locks on the Caldon branch *(Waterways News, British Waterways Board)*

of their undertaking. He drafted a specimen waybill, which listed places and distances and also included some imaginative comments: 'ı0 January 1783, Wincham, 2 miles. Stopt the boat all night, the captain being much in liquor and the boat damaged – He is in general a sober man – J. Ball.' Another entry declared that two crates had been broken open, but that for 12 January reported that 'the man who robbed the crates' had been detected and was in custody. The last entry read: '13 January Etruria Arrived, with 20 tons of clay – All well. E. Rochford.' Waybills of this type were in use in 1856, but the remarks for Fradley for the week ending 21 May were confined to 'Very wet' and 'Do. and windy'.

The 'Walking Surveyors' were also described in the *Commonplace Book*. They were to be 'the Ears and Eyes for the Committee, that is, for the Proprietors at large'. They had authority to examine all warehouses and wharfs, and to examine the waybill of every boat they met or overtook. They were to see that 'the men were sober and orderly' and report 'if there was any appearance of pilfering, and casks being plugged'. They were also to report any repairs needed to the canal, locks, towpaths or fences. The auditor's job was defined in similar detail, and great emphasis was placed on his personal responsibility; he might seek assistance from the clerks 'for the explanation of particulars', but should not yield up his 'own judgement to anyone'. The cashier was to have a room of his own 'with an iron chest for his cash and notes'. His work was described simply as receiving the company's cash, and keeping a cash account of receipts and expenditure. The work of the company's banker was dismissed quickly; his office was said to be 'little more than an iron chest'.

In August 1779 the canal between Stone and Middlewich was surveyed by Thomas Mills, J. Boyar and Josiah Wedgwood. They reported that 'the Locks and Bridges from Stoke to Etruria' were 'in good condition, better than most of those below', and that 'the Canal from Etruria to the south end of the tunnel' was 'in good condition, except in some parts of the towing path'. Many of the locks came in for criticism. At Hardings Wood, for example, the woodwork was 'close and good', but the bricks were 'very much decayed'.[8]

As the Weaver trustees had expected, their failure to ensure that the Trent & Mersey Canal terminated in the Weaver resulted

in a loss of traffic, especially of clay and flintstones going to
Winsford. In the five years ending 5 April 1778 clay shipped to
Winsford averaged 2,336 tons per annum, and flintstones averaged
357 tons per annum. In the next five years clay had fallen to 467
tons per annum, and flintstones to 210 tons per annum. Between
12 February 1778 and 14 December 1782 the Duke of Bridgewater's boats carried 21,745 crates of pottery from Preston Brook
to Liverpool. On the other hand there was a considerable reduction in the quantity of merchants' goods being shipped from
Winsford: this fell from 3,362 tons per annum in the five years
ending in 1778 to 515 tons per annum in the next five years.
Winsford had been the point of interchange between river and
land carriage for goods and materials passing between the Mersey
and the Potteries; after the opening of the canal, it lost much of
its trade. In the years 1777 to 1779, the following quantities of
flint and clay, in tons, were carried on the Trent & Mersey:

|                     | *1777* | *1778* | *1779* |
|---------------------|-------|-------|-------|
| Flints from Shardlow | 2516  | 2447  | 3233  |
| Flints from Burton  | 514   | 298   | 452   |
| Flints from Preston | 758   | 349   | 171   |
| Total               | 3788  | 3094  | 3856  |
|                     |       |       |       |
| Clay from Shardlow  | 916   | 961   | 1014  |
| Clay from Preston   | 5488  | 5843  | 4099  |
| Total               | 6404  | 6804  | 5113  |

At Northwich, where the canal and the river ran parallel to
each other below the town, trade on the Weaver was less severely
hit; but it declined from 103,618 tons per annum for the five
years ending 5 April 1778 to 95,496 tons per annum for the five
years after 1778. As Josiah Wedgwood had predicted, most of the
salt produced in Cheshire was still shipped down the Weaver, and
most of the coal for the Northwich area was still brought up
the river. Anxious to maintain this trade, the trustees tried to
improve their navigation and establish a connection between
the river and the canal. After a petition from the salt proprietors
of Liverpool and Northwich for a reduction in tonnage dues, a
general meeting of the trustees was held on 15 March 1788. The
meeting agreed that 'if proper quays with communications and
other convenience, were created and made at Anderton or Barnton

for reshipping of goods and merchandizes into the River Weaver from the Staffordshire Canal, it would be a more eligible plan for the benefit of trade on the Weaver than a reduction of tonnage'.

The plan for a connection was not taken up, but the trustees decided to repair the road from the canal at Broken Cross to the Weaver at the 'Guide Post in Penny Lane'. Land was bought at Broken Cross, and on 7 October 1779 the trustees ordered a warehouse to be built near the navigation timber-yard in Castle Northwich. This was to be used for goods which had been brought from the warehouse at Broken Cross and were to be transhipped on the Weaver. By 1780 the road and warehouse had been completed at a cost of £2,331. For the next four years the trustees attempted to organise the carriage of goods between Longport and Liverpool. A clerk was appointed at Longport whose job was to send the crates-ware down the canal to Broken Cross, where it would be transferred to the Weaver at Northwich. The trade was not profitable, and the concern was abandoned on 5 January 1784; the wharf, warehouse and cranes at Broken Cross were put up for sale. The road from Middlewich to Winsford, however, was repaired: in 1785 Josiah Wedgwood described it as 'an excellent gravel road'. Shipments of flintstones to Winsford continued on a considerable scale until 1794.

On 6 November 1788 the salt proprietors of Middlewich suggested to the trustees that quays and communications might be made at Anderton or Barnton, so that goods could be transferred from the Trent & Mersey Canal to the Weaver. The trustees accepted the idea, and two plans were put before the Trent & Mersey Co on 5 August 1790. One which involved a sluice across the towpath of the canal was rejected, while that which involved wheeling goods over the towpath was accepted. On 7 April 1791 the trustees began negotiations for the purchase of land adjoining the canal at Anderton. A crane was erected, and the salt proprietors of Middlewich were asked to give security that they would carry their salt to Liverpool by the proposed link. They agreed to give a security of £500.

A new basin was made on the river at Anderton to acommodate boats receiving goods from the canal. This basin ran parallel to the canal, and was linked with the river by a short cut. It was within 44yd of the canal, but there was no channel between the two. Initially carts were wheeled down the 50ft drop to the basin,

but in 1799 a 'railed Way' was built. This may perhaps have been
an inclined plane on which the empty wagons were hauled up by
the weight of the descending wagons. In 1813, at any rate, it was
reported that salt was transferred from the canal to the Weaver
by an 'inclined plane' at Anderton. In the 1790s the connection
was used for salt but not for clay or crates-ware. Between April
1795 and April 1800 17,674 tons of white salt from Middlewich
were shipped down the Weaver; these shipments were recorded
at Northwich.[9]

The carrying trade of the Trent & Mersey Canal was undertaken at first by a few private carriers. One of these was the
Cavendish Bridge Boat Co which, on 1 May 1780, advertised
wharfs and warehouses for sale on both sides of the canal at
Shardlow. The advertisement claimed that 'a very comfortable
business' had been carried on for several years at the wharfs, and
that the company had twenty boats 'employed fully' on the canal.
On 8 and 15 May 1781 the *Manchester Mercury* announced that 'all
land, Buildings, and equipment of the Cavendish Bridge Boat
Company' were to be put up for auction 'because of bankruptcy'.
Another firm of private carriers was known as Hugh Henshall &
Co; it retained this name even when the firm had been taken over
by the Trent & Mersey to prevent the forming of combinations
among the other carriers. It seemed logical to Wedgwood that the
canal company should act as carriers, since they wished to increase
their profits by carrying as much as possible at reasonable prices.

The company was prevented by law from varying the tolls for
any part of the canal, and had to give due notice of any reductions. This meant that the rate could not be lowered where there
was competition unless a general reduction was made. When the
canal company acted as carriers, however, they could lower the
freight charges 'in any degree or on any part of the canal', as
circumstances required. In the years 1783–4 charges were reduced
for iron, lead, copper, timber, glass-maker's sand, clay, flint,
crates of pottery ware, slates, corn, malt, ale, cheese and salt.

Hugh Henshall & Co and their owners the Trent & Mersey
Canal Co were confronted with a difficult situation in 1782. John
Gilbert, who was both agent to the Duke of Bridgewater and
one of the Trent & Mersey proprietors, entered into a partnership
with 'a considerable waggoner' named Worthington for carrying
goods by canal between Manchester and Stourport in competition

with the Trent & Mersey. The rumour was spread that Hugh Henshall & Co intended to give up the carriage of goods between Manchester and Stourport, but this was denied in the newspapers.

The 'amicable society' of proprietors was badly disrupted for a time by the row which developed between the Duke of Bridgewater, who had ordered his agent at Preston Brook to deliver all unconsigned goods for Stourport to Worthington & Gilbert, and Josiah Wedgwood, who with others was prepared to support a new carrying company between Preston Brook and Liverpool. This new company would carry all goods for 2s 4d per ton, whereas the Duke charged 3s 4d per ton; they would use river boats smaller than the Duke's, so that Cheshire cheese could be carried from Middlewich to Liverpool without the damage it sometimes received in transhipment.

A number of complaints against the Duke were presented by Caister, the Trent & Mersey's chief agent at Manchester, in a letter of 13 September 1783. Caister described the disturbance caused by Worthington's boats and continued: 'Worthington's boats and carts must be dispatched first, next his Graces business at our warehouses . . . I have only two porters allowed to my business, and those are not under my own direction, they are frequently called off to do Worthington's and his Graces business, when ours must stand still.' Caister brought many criticisms against Worthington, and objected to the partiality which 'His Graces people' showed towards him. When the letter was shown to the Duke he demanded Caister's dismissal, and on 7 January 1784 he threatened to dispose of his shares in the Trent & Mersey if this demand was not met. Undeterred, the committee of the Trent & Mersey uncovered 'partialities' shown to Worthington & Gilbert at Liverpool and Preston; in both places, they claimed, goods which should have been delivered to their boats had been given to their rivals.

In an undated letter to the other proprietors of the Trent & Mersey Canal Co, an 'old Proprietor' set out arguments against Josiah Wedgwood whom he described as the 'most active person' in this quarrel. The author claimed that the reduced rates of the 'New Company' were not what they seemed, and that they would not bring as much profit as was expected. He also argued that boats of the size used by the Duke were the most suitable and least expensive for the tideway of the Mersey.

The quarrel was related to complaints recorded in the Committee of Commerce minutes from the end of 1784 to October 1786; these referred to the lack of proper warehouses at Preston Brook for clay and flintstones and for crates of manufactured wares. On 29 March 1785 a memorial was laid before the General Assembly, in which it was claimed that two-thirds of the whole tonnage between Liverpool and the Potteries consisted of these items, and that the canal had sustained great loss because the warehouses at Preston quay were too small and there was insufficient room for storing clay. There was usually 1,000 to 1,500 tons of clay on the banks, but storage space for only 400–500 tons. The clay was often damaged, so that it was sometimes reduced by 10s per ton in value. On 21 December 1785 a similar complaint was made about the poor condition in which flintstones were brought to the Potteries.

William Jessop was evidently much impressed by the vehemence of the dispute. On 7 April 1785 he wrote from Newark to Martin, the superintendent of the Aire & Calder Canal:

> They have had violent Disputes among the Proprietors of the Grand Trunk Canal – and at the most numerous General Meeting which they have ever had, the Duke of Bridgewater & Lord Gower being present they have turned the most active Men of their old Committee (Mr. Wedgwood, Dr. Faulkner etc) & had a large majority in favour of a proposition to give up trading as a Company & I believe they mean to sell all their boats & let their warehouses.

On 26 September 1786 the committee of the Trent & Mersey passed a number of resolutions arising from these complaints. It was proposed that the freight charges for clay and flintstones between Liverpool and the Potteries should be reduced to the following:

|                                        | s  | d per ton |
|----------------------------------------|----|-----------|
| Between Liverpool and Longport Wharf   | 9  | 6         |
| Between Liverpool and Etruria Wharf    | 9  | 10        |
| Between Liverpool and Stoke Wharf      | 10 | 3         |

including the duties payable for tonnage and wharfage, and all other expenses. It was also suggested that additional cranes should be erected at the wharfs mentioned, so as to reduce the breakages, and that an agent should be stationed at these wharfs to assist in unloading and reloading the goods.

The quarrel was still continuing in 1788. A notice inserted in the *Manchester Mercury* for 1 April complained that country carriers who brought goods to Manchester to be forwarded by Henshall & Co had been delivering them to 'other persons'. This had proved injurious to Henshall & Co, 'as well as the Publick', and carriers were warned, 'on Pain of Prosecution', not to deliver goods contrary to order. Anyone who gave 'Information of Goods being so delivered' would be 'liberally rewarded' if he applied to 'Mr Hebbert at Castle Quay'.

The outcome of the dispute seems to have been a compromise. The Duke became more co-operative in his dealings with the Trent & Mersey Canal Co and did not carry out his threat to sell his shares. The Trent & Mersey, on the other hand, neither gave up their carrying concern nor implemented their proposal for a 'new company' to handle trade between Preston Brook and Liverpool.[10]

Josiah Wedgwood died on 3 January 1795 at Etruria Hall and was buried in Stoke-on-Trent. The obituary in the *Gentleman's Magazine* praised him not only for his contribution to the pottery industry, but also for the 'greatness of mind' which enabled him to promote the Trent & Mersey Canal. In October 1795, a few months after his death, a 'Friend to the Improvement of his Country' wrote that 'the improvement and extent of the Potteries was almost wholly owing to the convenience of water-conveyance' and that 'the lands near the Staffordshire Canals' had been 'greatly improved and rapidly advanced in value by their means, and by the consequent increase of trade'. The writer declared that the 'honest and industrious poor' had lost in Wedgwood a 'kind and generous benefactor'. Wedgwood's numerous extant letters reveal him to have been energetic, kind, tolerant, intelligent and realistic. He was indeed a benefactor to the poor, but he was far from sentimental in his attitude to them, as is shown by the letter he wrote to his brother John on 7 August 1765: 'I am just teazed out of my life with dilatory drunken idle workmen which prevents my proceeding in the tea service, to which more sorts of workmen are necessary than one would imagine.' After the death of his partner Thomas Bentley in 1780, Josiah's nephew, Thomas Byerley, had become a partner, and from 1790 the firm was known

as 'Wedgwood Sons & Byerley'. Josiah had adopted Byerley, and
on 28 May 1764 he described him as 'a very good boy', and expressed the hope that he would make 'a usefull member of society'.
Byerley had eight daughters; in 1809 three of them set up a 'very
good and flourishing school' at Warwick. The school later moved
to Barford where one of its pupils was Elizabeth Stevenson,
whose family was connected with the Wedgwoods. Some of the
novels she wrote later as Elizabeth Gaskell were set in Manchester
and Cheshire.

As Wedgwood's commitment to high standards of efficiency
ensured the durability of his pottery firm, so it contributed also
to the success of the Trent & Mersey Canal. As Flaxman's
Monument to his memory said, 'he converted a rude and incon-
siderable manufactory into an elegant art and an important part
of commerce'. He also made a large fortune, and left over
£500,000.[11]

Wedgwood's death was followed by that of John Gilbert on 4
August 1795. Thomas Gilbert died in 1798, but the Duke of
Bridgewater continued active until 1803. All these pioneers had
lived to see the success of the undertakings they had promoted
and developed.

All but three of the Trent & Mersey shares were paid up in
1773; but during the lean years from 1771 to 1780 no interest was
paid on the calls. The unpaid interest on calls from 18 September
1775 to 18 March 1780 was £45 for each £200 share and amounted
to £29,250; in 1783 Parliament granted authority for bonds to
be given for this amount. In 1782 there were 240 shareholders,
many of whom were also mortgagees; 47 of them had been among
the original 101 proprietors in 1766. By the act of 1802 (42 Geo
III c 25) the original 650 shares at £200 each were subdivided to
make 1300 shares at £100 each. No person was to hold more than
50 shares. Dividends were paid from 23 June 1781, when it was
announced that dividends would be 2½ per cent half-yearly at
'Midsummer and Christmas' till further notice. The surplus
profits were to be applied to the payment of the company's
debts.[12]

The dividend paid on 23 July 1783 was 3⅛ per cent, and that
paid on 25 December of the same year was 2½ per cent. For the
half-year from 19 June to 19 December 1784, the dividend was
2½ per cent. In 1786 the committee apologised for not increasing

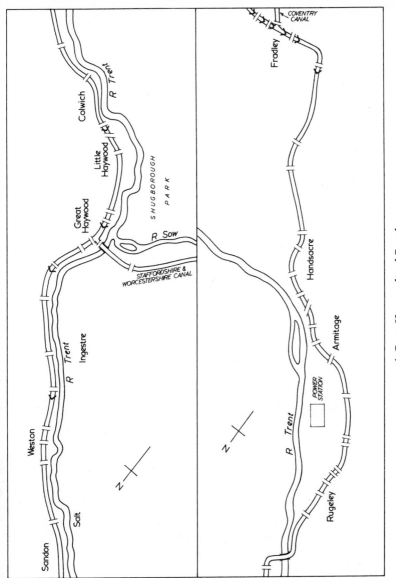

6 Great Haywood and Rugeley

the dividends, which were then presumably 5 per cent; they explained that they had built the section of the Coventry Canal between Whittington Brook and Fradley without borrowing additional funds, and they expressed the hope that the proprietors would not consider this an 'improper Appropriation of their surplus Profits'. In 1787 the dividend was again 5 per cent. This was because the company had built reservoirs, wharfs, quays and warehouses which were necessary for the 'prosperity of Trade'. The dividend was increased to 5½ per cent in 1788, to 6 per cent in 1789, and to 6½ per cent in 1790.[13]

After the completion of construction work and the paying of debts, the dividends continued to increase as long as the carrying trade flourished. In 1806 the £100 shares were selling at £840 and the dividend per annum was 40 per cent. The share prices fluctuated from month to month, but the dividends rose from 40 per cent in 1810 to 75 per cent in 1820 and stayed at that figure until 1831. By an act of 1827 (7 & 8 Geo IV c 81) the £100 shares were subdivided into 2,600 shares of £50 each. No person was allowed to hold more than 100 shares. The following table shows the share prices and dividends for the years 1810–31:[14]

| Date | Share price (£) | Dividend (per cent per annum) |
|------|-----------------|-------------------------------|
| 1810 | 1,050–1,075 | 40 |
| 1811 | 1,150–1,260 | 45 |
| 1812 | 1,047–1,110 | 47½ |
| 1813 | 1,180 | 50 |
| 1814 | 1,220–1,230 | 55 |
| 1815 | 1,165–1,265 | 55 |
| 1816 | 1,225 | 60 |
| 1817 | 1,250–1,414 | 60 |
| 1818 | 1,530–1,600 | 65 |
| 1819 | not known | — |
| 1820 | 1,875–1,920 | 75 |
| 1821 | 1,790–1,999 | 75 |
| 1822 | 1,800–1,999 | 75 |
| 1823 | 2,000 | 75 |
| 1824 | 2,200–2,400 | 75 |
| 1825 | 2,100–2,200 | 75 |
| 1826 | 1,800–2,000 | 75 |
| 1827 | 1,600–1,850 | 75 |

| 1828 | 1,620–1,650 | 75 |
| 1829 | 1,580–1,590 | 75 |
| 1830 | 1,200–1,560 | 75 |
| 1831 | 1,200–1,500 | 75 |

It would appear that share prices reached their peak in 1824, with £2,400 as the highest price recorded. An unspecified bonus was paid in the years 1824, 1826 and 1827.

J. R. Ward has concluded, on the evidence of the surviving transfer records, that the rate at which shares changed hands depended on the circumstances of the time and the prospects of the company. A document in Birmingham Central Library describes a deed of transfer dated 5 May 1785 by which John Pybus, at the request of Charles Simpson of Lichfield, was paid £1,000 by Phoebe Simpson for his five shares in the Trent & Mersey Canal Co. This indicates that at that date the value of the shares was at par. On 27 November 1792, however, Josiah Wedgwood sold a half-share in the Trent & Mersey to the Right Honourable Harrowby for £500, which shows that the value of the canal stock was rising fast. On 24 September 1793 the *Manchester Mercury* advertised shares which were to be sold by the proprietors at the Annual General Meeting. On 13 January 1823 'Mr. Scott' of Blackfriars in London advertised in *Aris's Birmingham Gazette* a share in the 'excellent Navigation from the Trent to the Mersey'. The advertisement gave the dividend as '£75 per annum', and continued: 'The eminent merits of this long-established prosperous concern are well-known. The dividends are regularly paid in January and July in London, forming a most eligible fund for family investment.' At that date Mr Scott could expect a price of £2,000.[15]

The surviving accounts for the period from 14 June to 27 December 1783 show that traffic was heavier in the second half of that period, and illustrate the range of goods which the canal carried:[16]

| Goods | Tolls from 14 June to 13 September (£) | Tolls from 13 September to 27 December (£) |
| --- | --- | --- |
| Crates of pottery | 587 | 698 |
| Clay | 541 | 692 |
| Lime and limestone (Caldon branch) | 515 | 388 |

| | | |
|---|---|---|
| Grain, meal and flour | 456 | 391 |
| Salt | 326 | 346 |
| Harecastle coal | 296 | 350 |
| Timber, plank and boards | 259 | 478 |
| Flint | 249 | 379 |
| Iron | 184 | 314 |
| Groceries | 158 | 424 |
| Nails | 89 | 147 |
| Cheese | 72 | 204 |

In the period from February to December 1789, Josiah
Wedgwood's firm paid £1,034 in freight charges to Hugh
Henshall & Co. The principal goods transported were crates of
earthenware passing from Etruria to Liverpool, Gainsborough,
Stourport or Birmingham, and loads of clay passing from Liverpool to Etruria. Other cargoes included '12 Hogsheads porter'
which were carried from Gainsborough to Etruria on 9 May.[17]

Tonnage revenue from 27 June to 25 December 1773 was
£2,247, and the carrying profit for this period was £417. The net
profit to 14 June 1781 was £93,282. The net profit for the year
ending 14 June 1782 was £21,896, and for the year ending 14
June 1783 it was £19,038. The net profit on the Caldon branch
to 14 June 1783 was £2,719.

From 1784 to 1815 the income from tolls increased steadily,
but there was no comparable increase in carrying profits:[18]

| Year, ending June | Tolls (£) | Carrying profit (£) | Total (£) |
|---|---|---|---|
| 1784 | 23,152 | 1,272 | 24,424 |
| 1785 | 26,054 | 3,859 | 29,913 |
| 1786 | 26,964 | 1,522 | 28,486 |
| 1787 | 28,459 | 2,780 | 31,239 |
| 1788 | 30,362 | 2,995 | 33,357 |
| 1789 | 33,861 | 3,079 | 36,940 |
| 1790 | 36,950 | 5,108 | 42,058 |
| 1791 | 40,773 | 5,084 | 45,857 |
| 1792 | 42,505 | 3,681 | 46,186 |
| 1802 (June–December) | 36,253 | 836 | 37,089 |
| 1812 | 107,475 | 2,722 | 110,197 |
| 1815 | 123,707 | 2,409 | 126,116 |

Hugh Henshall died at Longport in 1817, but the carrying
trade with which his name was associated continued to be

operated by the Trent & Mersey Co until the late 1840s.

The boats used by the long-distance carriers were built of wood and were relatively light. There was a cabin at the rear, and the design scarcely changed until the railway era. Railway competition resulted in a loss of general goods traffic, and the boats were then built with a hull of squarer cross-section, which made them more suitable for the transport of bulk cargoes. An early description of a canal boat can be found in the Wedgwood Collection. It was written at Etruria on 31 July 1786, and it lays down conditions for the building of a new boat. It was to be 68ft long at bottom and 6ft 10in wide 'from outside to outside'. The sides were to be 'rounded 4in', and a 'false bottom' was to be laid 'crossways at the Foredeck' to prevent water from 'washing into the boat in going through the locks'. The cabin was to have a 'high top or roof and bedsides and two cupboards besides the stern cupboard and two shelves'. The helm was to be in one piece, and the boat was to be 'in every respect completed in a good and workmanlike manner for 14½ guineas'.

The newspapers reported numerous 'melancholy incidents' connected with the canal. Many were the result of drunkenness, which could make a walk along the towpath very hazardous. A particularly macabre accident was reported by the *Doncaster Gazette* on 17 February 1813. The victim was Benjamin Dyke, who was 'in the employ of Messrs. Pickford and Co', and the manner of his death was described as follows:

> As he was driving a horse along the towing path of the Grand Trunk Canal, near Rugeley, on the night of the 23rd ult, the horse became unruly, and the rope by which he drew the boat, unfortunately broke, and striking against the boatman, was twirled by the force of the jerk several times round his body; in this situation the poor fellow was dragged by the horse, sometimes in the canal, and sometimes on the towing path, till the rope at length broke, and left him in the water, where he was found dead in a short time afterwards.

A verdict of accidental death was recorded.

In 1812 a carrying company known as Sutton, Robinson & Co was operating both on the River Trent and on the Trent & Mersey and Bridgewater Canals; they handled traffic for 'Shard-low, Manchester, Liverpool, the Cheshire Saltworks, the Staffordshire Potteries and all intermediate Places'; and they also advertised as 'General Wharfingers at Shardlow'. In 1831 they were known as the James Sutton & Shardlow Boat Co, and in 1852 they were still based in Shardlow; but in 1857 they retired from the carrying trade. One company that survived the railway age was the Anderton Co, which had begun trading as Alexander Reid & Co but changed its name in 1836 when it took over the transhipment trade at Anderton.

In 1829–30 the Weaver trustees had greatly enlarged the transhipment basins at Anderton, and had built two entrances. In 1832 a new inclined plane was built for the conveyance of coal, and later salt and other goods, passing between the river and the canal. Early in 1835 Alexander Reid & Co were allowed to construct their own rails for the transhipment of timber, and on 25 June of the same year, in response to an application from this company, the engineer and solicitor of the Trent & Mersey reached agreement with the Weaver trustees over the construction of a new towpath on the eastern bank of the canal opposite the Anderton basin. The trustees undertook to make the necessary bridges, but they stipulated that if the old towpath was ever reopened, the cost of building these bridges would be repaid by the Trent & Mersey.

During the 1840s most of the white salt from Cheshire was sent down the Weaver. The tonnage being shipped from Winsford increased steadily between 1840 and 1870, as is shown in the following table:

| Year ending April | From Northwich | From Winsford |
|---|---|---|
| 1840 | 245,075 | 169,081 |
| 1850 | 283,146 | 324,250 |
| 1860 | 274,934 | 420,830 |
| 1870 | 261,003 | 640,155 |

The Anderton Co continued to operate until 1954, when the business was sold to the Mersey Weaver & Ship Canal Carrying Co. It survived so long because its boats worked short journeys, and because much of its cargo consisted of crates of pottery which manufacturers preferred to send by canal.[19]

As the point of transhipment between the Trent & Mersey and the River Trent, Shardlow developed into a prosperous and attractive inland port. It was bounded on the south by the Trent and on the east by the Derwent. The original settlement was a hamlet of the royal manor of Weston-on-Trent, and was situated at the northern end of Shardlow. Wilden Ferry or Wilne Ferry developed as a crossing-place on the south bank of the Trent in the sixteenth century. The ferry was replaced by Cavendish Bridge, which was authorised in 1758 and opened in 1761; the bridge cost £3,333, and high tolls were charged in order to pay for it. Shardlow, which lay between these two settlements, was created by the canal. The Hon. John Byng visited Shardlow in June 1789. He noted that there were built around the canal 'so many merchants houses, wharfs, &c, sprinkled with gardens, looking upon the Trent, and to Castle Donington Hill, as to form as happy a scenery of business and pleasures as can be survey'd'.

Shardlow had many fine warehouses. One, dated 1794, was built over an arm of the canal and had low, wide-arched bays into which boats could be hauled. A malt-house, dated 1799, had a projecting gable slanting inwards to facilitate the loading and unloading of barrels. After about 1785, when men ceased to haul boats on the Trent, stable accommodation was provided for more than a hundred horses. On top of the stables a lantern was hung at night to guide barges. Unfortunately these stables have now been demolished. Substantial houses were built for the merchants and carriers, who included the Suttons, the Soresbys and the Flacks. In the early nineteenth century most of the traffic at Shardlow was controlled by James Sutton and John Soresby, both from local families. The offices of Stevens & Co are said to have been designed for John Soresby by Capability Brown (1715–83) but this seems unlikely.

Shardlow's trade in coal, limestone, freestone, gypsum, bar-iron, Derbyshire lead, pottery, ale, cheese, deal, pig-iron from Scandinavia, flint, chert, malt and barley earned it locally the name of 'little Liverpool'. Boats returned to Shardlow with cotton from Manchester, which was transhipped to the Trent and sent to Nottingham. After 1811, boats conveyed goods from Shardlow to Derby, Market Harborough, Hull, Sleaford, Lough-borough, Leicester, Nottingham, Grantham, Lincoln, Newark, Boston, Gainsborough, Horncastle, Manchester and Melton Mowbray, and to all places on the line of the Trent & Mersey and Bridgewater Canals. The fly-boats of the James Sutton & Shard-low Boat Co left every day, while those of John Soresby and

William Flack left four times a week.

The Suttons lived in Shardlow Hall, which is now owned by the Ministry of Agriculture. In 1684 the Hall was owned by Leonard Fosbrooke, whose family had moved from Wollaton to Shardlow about 1600 and had been concerned with the Trent Navigation for many years. By the 1690s Fosbrooke controlled Wilden Ferry, which had largely displaced Nottingham as the head of the Trent Navigation; he had also become an important river carrier, his principal cargo being cheese. The act of 1699 extended river navigation from Wilden Ferry to Burton-on-Trent, and in 1710 Fosbrooke made an agreement with George Hayne of Wirksworth, a river carrier engaged in the salt trade, by which Fosbrooke and Hayne were to share equally any contracts made with Lord Paget, or with anyone else concerned in the Trent Navigation.

By 1712 Burton had become head of the navigation. The Upper Trent provided transport for cheese and other goods from the Midlands, while iron, tar, hemp, flax, timber and corn were carried upstream from Hull and Gainsborough. The Haynes and the Fosbrookes maintained their control of the Upper Trent Navigation until 1760, when the Earl of Uxbridge sold the lease of the stretch from Burton to Wilden to a group of merchants and manufacturers. In 1783 the Trent Navigation Co was established, with authority to make and maintain the navigation on the Trent between Wilden Ferry and Gainsborough. After the completion of the canal from Shardlow to Great Haywood, the use of the Trent above Wilden declined rapidly; and Shardlow's population rose from 580 in 1801 to 1,306 in 1841. The canal took boats of 40 tons burden as far as Horninglow (Burton), and after 1790 it provided customers for a number of canal pubs such as the Navigation, the Shakespeare and the Crown. The building now occupied by the Malt Shovel Inn was built in 1799 as a house for the manager of the adjacent warehouse; but the name it was given when it became an inn had previously been that of an old inn in the village. At Shardlow in May 1839, 140 boatmen petitioned the Trent & Mersey Canal Co to close the canal on Sunday.[20]

In the Potteries, the owners of potworks built paths down to the canal-side from their warehouses and from collecting centres in the villages and towns. A number of wharfs were established:

*Plate 9*  The Hazelhurst aqueduct *(Waterways News, British Waterways Board)*

*Plate 10*  The Holly Bush Inn at Denford *(Waterways News, British Waterways Board)*

*Plate 11*   Josiah Wedgwood's factory at Etruria *(Messrs Josiah Wedgwood & Sons Ltd)*

*Plate 12*   The Colwich lock *(Harry Arnold)*

in 1802 these included the Grand Trunk Canal Wharfs at Longport, Etruria and Stoke; the wharfs of William Kenwright at
Longport, Shelton and Stoke; and the wharfs of John Brassington
and the Barton Boat Co at Stoke. By 1781 there was a wharf at
Tunstall Bridge, and a 'New Wharf' at Tunstall was referred to
in *White's Directory of Staffordshire* in 1834. By 1863 Tunstall had
nineteen potworks, one of which was on the canal. By about
1840 there were four public wharfs and several private wharfs in
Longport.[21]

In 1778 the 'average rates of freights upon the Canals' were 3d
per ton per mile for perishable goods and 2½d per ton per mile for
non-perishable goods. On the Duke of Bridgewater's Canal the
rates were 2s 6d per ton from Preston to Stockton Quay near
Warrington and 5s per ton from Preston to Manchester. The
rates on 'River Navigations' included 10s per ton from Shardlow
to Gainsborough, 10s per ton from Stourport to Bristol and 3s 4d
per ton from Preston to Liverpool. Charges for the carriage of
perishable goods from Liverpool included 2s 5d per ton to Hull,
2s 2d per ton to Bristol, and 3s per ton to London via Gainsborough. Charges for the carriage of non-perishable goods from
Liverpool included 2s 3d per ton to Hull, 1s 11d per ton to Bristol,
and 1s 11d per ton to Gainsborough.[22]

The Trent & Mersey Canal Co displayed their patriotism during
the Napoleonic Wars when, in April 1798, the proprietors gave
£1,000 for the 'defence of the realm'. On 3 July of the same year,
the *Manchester Mercury* reported a military use of the canal: 'The
residents near the banks of the Staffordshire Canal were on
Saturday and Sunday se'nnight pleasingly surprized by the
Marquis of Buckingham's regiment of Militia being taken along
in boats, on their way to Ireland. They were conveyed in this
manner to Runcorn and from thence to Liverpool in flats . . .
The Warwickshire Militia have been sent to Ireland in the same
manner.' The soldiers were evidently being sent to Ireland to put
down Wolfe Tone's rebellion. On 22 September another con-
tingent of soldiers on their way to Ireland was given a warm
welcome as they travelled by canal, and this event was recorded
by the *Staffordshire Advertiser*.[23]

In 1806 a plan was proposed for varying the line of the Trent &
Mersey through the hill at Harecastle: the new line was to run
north of Brindley's tunnel, passing close to the 'Bath Houses' and

slightly above 'Mr Gilbert's New Hall'. This plan was not carried out, but the company did implement an associated plan for a new and straighter line 28 chains 63 links in length near Lawton. Another abortive plan of the same year was for a tram-road from coal-works near Hardings Wood to the canal at the Lawton treble locks. The landowners on the route included Hugh Henshall, and the total length of the intended tram-road was 157 chains 68 links.[24]

The Hon. John Byng visited the Potteries in June 1792. In Stoke-on-Trent, he saw 'many pleasant villas for the principal merchants'. He observed the 'intersecting canals, with their passing boats, their bridges, the population, the pottery ovens, and the bustle of business'; and he declared the whole scene to be like a Chinese picture, where the angler was 'momentarily inter-rupted by a boat'. He regarded Stoke as a village, but said that Hanley had become 'a great town'. At Etruria he saw Wedg-wood's house, which was built of 'staring red brick'; and he was shown the 'great pottery', where 300 workers were employed.

In 1816 the fiftieth anniversary of the start of the Trent & Mersey Canal was celebrated in Burslem by all the 'respectable manufacturers', who assembled to pay tribute to Josiah Wedg-wood. By that date the Potteries were famous and had developed their distinctive personality. In 1818, a journalist declared that the region offered 'a scene of a novel kind totally different from the general character of an English town'. He was confused by the contrast between Etruria Hall and its surroundings: 'a large house, built of the finest materials, furnished in the most superb manner, and apparently better adapted for the palace of a grandee than the modest mansion of a tradesman; surrounded with furn-aces, kilns and sheds, and perpetually involved in smoke'. The account continued:

> Etruria . . . is the only place in the Potteries that has any pre-tension to beauty or even regularity. The sole property of Mr. Wedgwood – he built this village as one long street and numbered every dwelling. His manufactory he placed at the end contiguous to the canal and fixed his residence in the part adjoining. Thus, like the Baron of feudal times, he lived among his vassals, revered as a parent, respected by his chief.

The Hall remained in the possession of the Wedgwood family

until 1851; in the 1850s it was sold to the Duchy of Lancaster, and in 1860 it was let to Earl Granville, who had established a branch of the Shelton ironworks on a site to the west of the Hall.

In 1879 Henry Wedgwood published a series of sketches about Staffordshire; in one of these he described the park of Etruria Hall, 'a beautiful undulating greenness before the Hall of the great potter'. He referred to the ornamental water in front of the Hall, and to the winter scene 'when the canal and the hall pool . . . were frozen over, and the trees looked so picturesque'. Even an ice-boat seemed to him romantic, as it came 'dashing and swaying along, drawn by ten or a dozen horses at the gallop'. He recalled an occasion when another ice-boat, with 'about fifteen horses and 30 or 40 men', had cleared the ice from the ice-bound canal; Francis Wedgwood had then attempted to take a short cut across the canal from the Hall to the works, and had 'stepped up to the middle in water'.[25]

The canal's influence was also felt in Stone, where it ran parallel to the High Street throughout the length of the town. At Meaford, beyond the town, the canal originally climbed up by means of a staircase of three riser locks followed by a single lock. In the 1820s the canal line was altered so that the old loop was cut off and the canal proceeded in a straight easterly direction with three new and separate locks. Above Meaford top lock a cast-iron milepost bore the inscription 'R & D Stone 1819'. This milepost was probably cast in the iron foundry of Rangeley & Dixon in Lichfield Street, Stone. The town was a busy centre for canal traffic, and about 700 boats a week passed along the canal in its heyday. The old canal-side brewery has now been demolished, but the Star Inn at Stone bottom lock still exists, and the town has two boatyards and three dry docks.[26]

The period immediately after Waterloo was one of depression in agriculture and trade, and the Trent & Mersey's trade in limestone and grain was particularly affected. On 17 October 1820 the committee reported to the General Assembly that there had been a 'falling off in the tolls'; but the matter was not considered very serious, as the canal had been stopped by ice for five weeks and had been wholly unproductive during that time. The committee also informed the assembly that an additional tunnel had been recommended at Harecastle, and that a survey and report by John Rennie had placed the need for such a tunnel 'almost . . .

beyond a doubt'. The tunnel had been a source of complaint for many years, as it slowed down traffic and was seriously in need of repair. In 1820, however, railway competition was not yet an immediate threat. The committee decided that the tunnel was 'not a case of immediate urgency', and that 'mature deliberation' should be given to the question.

In his report, Rennie commented on the low roof of the tunnel, the poor state of the brickwork, and the condition of the side-tunnels which communicated with the coal-works; and he offered three possible solutions to the problem. His first proposal was a thorough repair of the existing tunnel. He suggested that while this was proceeding 'a Railway might be laid across the Hill and the Cargoes of the Boats might be unloaded at each end of the Tunnel and transported across the Hill'. This plan would involve two inclined planes and two steam-engines, and would be the cheapest and most rapid scheme; but loading and discharging the cargoes at the ends of the inclined planes would 'occasion much detention, damage and loss of property, as well as a heavy expense'. Nor was this the only objection: 'when the repairs of the Tunnel were completed, the bulk of the expense incurred in the formation of the railway and inclined planes would in great measure be lost'.

Rennie's second proposal was for a new tunnel; this would cost some £58,000, 'but when done its benefits would be great and permanent'. The construction of a new tunnel would make it possible to repair the old one; and the existence of two tunnels would 'give great dispatch to the Trade, as all the Boats passing one way might go by one Tunnel, and thus the stoppage by the present Tunnel of three hours for the alternate passage of Boats would be avoided'. Rennie's third proposal was that the tunnel should be bypassed by an 'open cut with 16 locks through Bath Pool Valley'. He estimated the initial cost of this plan at £57,000, inclusive of steam-engines and shafts, and the annual cost of the steam-engines, inclusive of fuel, engineers and repairs, at £3,066; and he pointed out that such a scheme 'would not be so complete or expeditious as a second Tunnel'. He concluded by saying that a second tunnel would promote trade and remove 'the temptation to the making of other lines of canal in opposition to the Grand Trunk'.[27]

Rennie also carried out, in company with the committee's

chairman James Caldwell, and the surveyor and resident engineer James Potter, an inspection of Rudyard Reservoir. Rennie recommended either an alteration of the feeder from the River Dane or a diversion into the reservoir of surplus waters from the River Churnet; if necessary, he said, the surplus waters of both rivers could be diverted into new reservoirs created to receive them. He examined the site at Knypersley, where the company proposed to build a new reservoir; but he was not disposed to support this plan, since he believed that it would be better to improve existing supplies.[28] The company decided on 25 April 1821 to present a bill to Parliament to enable them to make an additional tunnel through Harecastle Hill, and to allow them to make a reservoir in Knypersley valley and improve the feeder from the River Dane. The unexpected death of Rennie, however, made them decide in December 1821 to postpone the bill to another year, and it was not obtained until 1823. The committee's report for 1821 ended on an optimistic note with a statement that the trade upon the canal was reviving and should continue to improve.[29]

Thomas Telford was chosen to succeed Rennie as consultant engineer. On 25 March 1822, he made his report to the Trent & Mersey Navigation on the River Dane feeder, the proposed reservoir at Knypersley and the Harecastle tunnel. Telford's comments were concise and decisive. He had found 'no symptoms of immediate danger of failure' in the tunnel; but he said that the crown of the arch was too low, that the tunnel was in several parts too low and too narrow, and that 'long experience' had shown it to be 'quite inadequate for the business transacted'. Two hours were allowed for the passage, and large numbers of boats had to wait their turn; and so, 'notwithstanding strict regulations, much contention and confusion took place'. Telford was in no doubt that the 'only effectual remedy' was an additional tunnel. This would save 'much time, trouble and expense', and would 'render unnecessary the attendance of many Extra men who must occasionally be a great nuisance'.

Telford recommended that the new tunnel be made on the eastern side of the old tunnel, with about 25 yd between them. He considered that the new tunnel would then be in undisturbed ground, drained by the old tunnel, and clear of the coal workings. He estimated the cost at about £60,000. His advice on the

Dane feeder was that the banks towards the upper end should be raised, and that the bottom of the channel should be sunk towards the lower end. This would correct the feeder's defect of being almost level, and would give it a fall of 9 or 10ft.

Telford commented favourably on the proposed site for an additional reservoir at Knypersley, saying that it could use the same feeders as the adjacent reservoir at Rudyard and could be inspected at the same time.[30] In 1823 the company obtained an act (4 Geo IV c 87) for a reservoir at Knypersley and a tunnel about 2,800yd long. The tunnel was to be built within ten years, and a toll of 1½d per ton per mile was authorised. The company was empowered to raise £60,000 on a mortgage. On 2 June 1824 James Caldwell wrote to Telford expressing the committee's 'great satisfaction' in having placed responsibility for the new tunnel, the proposed Knypersley Reservoir and the improvement of the Dane feeder in Telford's hands. Telford was to be assisted by a resident engineer, who would 'reside constantly upon the spot for the purpose of overlooking and reporting . . . upon the state and progress of the work'; and James Potter was appointed to this post.[31] A postscript to Caldwell's letter gave a hint of the new dangers which the proprietors now faced: 'Is the Canal Navigation to be ruined by these *Rail Road* Projectors? If so, Canal Proprietors had better stop all further improvements, and then, what will soon be the state of the Country?'

On 5 July 1824 Telford recommended that the new tunnel should have a towpath about 4ft 6in wide. This meant that the whole width of the tunnel would be 14ft, and that the expense would be increased by one-sixth or one-seventh; but Telford was confident that 'the facilities afforded by a free passage to the Boatmen and Horses would much more than compensate this additional expense'. On the same date Telford recommended that the existing tunnel should be widened and equipped with a towpath. This suggestion was never carried out; but the general committee, meeting at Stone on 11 July, decided unanimously in favour of a towpath in the new tunnel.[32] These decisions meant that the new tunnel allowed traffic to pass in one direction only, and that leggers continued to operate in the old tunnel.

In 1824 the cost of building a new tunnel 2,900yd long and 16ft high was estimated at £82,474 and on 9 May 1825 Telford informed Potter that his salary as resident engineer would be not less than £500 per annum.[33] The work of building the tunnel, as Telford described it in a report, involved the laying of railways from the brick and mortar yards to the shafts and inclined planes near the north end, and the erection of steam-engines to pump out water and remove earth at the north and south ends of the tunnel. On the summit of the tunnel line there were houses, stables and workshops for the workmen and the horses; these saved time and avoided unnecessary exposure in bad weather. Fifteen shafts were to be sunk, and Telford hoped that the tunnel would be opened, as planned, 'by the latter end of the year 1827'.[34]

Writing to Potter on 7 July, Telford advised against side-tunnels from the coal-workings into the new tunnel; he argued that these would be troublesome and risky to construct, and that they would cause interruptions to trade.[35] On 3 October 1836 Potter told Telford that all but 112⅔ yds of the tunnel had been completed, and that the contractor David Pritchard expected to complete the paving of the towpath in two months.[36] According to Rickman, the tunnel was opened on 30 April 1827. The original estimate of £82,474 had been exceeded by at least £32,900.

On 3 November 1827 James Potter sent Telford an account of various works not taken into consideration in Telford's original report: the towpath had cost an extra £9,600; brick-making equipment and labour had cost an extra £4,300; railways and wagons had cost an extra £7,000; and £12,000 extra had been needed to make the tunnel wide enough to permit a towpath to be constructed. Other factors causing extra cost had been the nature of the ground, which was extremely hard, and 'the Quick island' at the north end, which had needed draining. The railway had been necessary in order to speed up the work; and for the same purpose the number of shafts had been doubled.[37]

On 21 March 1829, after carrying out a thorough inspection, Telford reported to the company on the state of the tunnel. He had walked along the towpath, examining the work very carefully by means of a lantern and candle. After being worked for two years, the tunnel appeared to him 'quite perfect'; throughout its length, which was 2,926yd, there were no cracks or decayed bricks. Telford praised James Potter's accuracy in setting out the line, and paid tribute to the contractor David Pritchard and his assistant and son-in-law William Hoof.[38] Writing to Caldwell on

7 April 1829, Telford again expressed his complete satisfaction with the work. He declared it to be 'the most perfect Work of its kind yet executed' and said that the sum of £118,000 had been 'laudably expended in accomplishing so useful a Work in so short a time'. He argued that any attempt at economy would have caused delay, produced 'superficial work' and 'incurred a risk of serious accidents'. He had asked a boatman coming out of the tunnel how he found it, and had received the reply, 'I only wish that it reached all the way to Manchester!'[39]

Knypersley Reservoir was situated at the bottom of a valley where there was alluvial matter to a great depth. This made it very difficult to establish a firm foundation for an embankment of the size needed. On 8 September 1828 George E. Hamilton, a civil engineer from Stone, made a report on the masonry at the reservoir. He said that the masonry was fractured in some places near the well, and that the discharge pipes were defective. On 21 November 1828 James Potter gave an account of the construction of the reservoir, which had been started in January 1825. He explained that difficulties with one landowner, Mr Bateman, had held up the progress of the work for over two years, and that another, Mr Williamson, had threatened 'to bring all his colliers and eject us by main force'. Potter was annoyed that after complaints about the pipes some members of the canal company had inspected the reservoir without consulting him or his father. A special committee of the General Assembly had asked James Trubshaw to deal with the matter of the pipes, and according to Potter it was Trubshaw's methods which had caused them to be fractured. Potter pointed out that he had not visited the site until the committee sent for him, and concluded that the matter was out of his hands. On 24 November 1828 Potter wrote to Telford, criticising members of the company for engaging Trubshaw to take measurements at the reservoir. James Trubshaw (1777–1853) was later responsible for the controversial Grosvenor Bridge over the River Dee at Chester. On 7 December 1828 Potter wrote to Telford again, saying that he wished to leave the service of the Trent & Mersey Canal Co.

On 11 December 1828 James Caldwell sent instructions to Telford about the reservoir, and about the need to protect Mr. Williamson's land by making a drain. George Hamilton was another victim of the quarrel about the reservoir. On 24 January

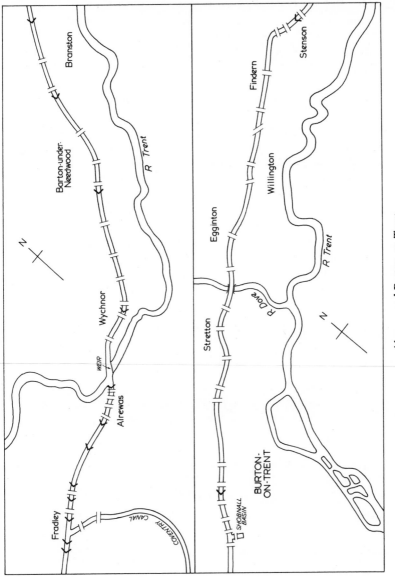

7 Alrewas and Burton-on-Trent

1829 he complained to Telford that he had been accused of making erroneous measurements, and continued: 'I must say I wish I never had had anything to do with the business. Like the old man in the fable I tried to please everybody and have met with precisely similar success.' As late as 12 September 1829 William Vaughan of Stone was writing to Telford about the imperfect nature of the reservoir, where water had escaped through the masonry because the discharging pipes were not watertight.[40]

By 1829 the Trent & Mersey's trade was being threatened by a number of rival projects. The Cromford & High Peak Railway had been authorised in 1825 and was to be opened in 1831. The Birmingham & Liverpool Junction Canal (now the Shropshire Union Main Line) had been authorised in 1826 and was to be opened in 1835. The Middlewich branch of the Ellesmere & Chester Canal had been promoted in 1827; and the Macclesfield Canal was to be opened in 1831. This competition had serious effects, and in 1830 there was another threat to the company's London, Liverpool and Manchester trade. This came from the proposal for a canal from the Stratford-on-Avon Canal to the Grand Junction at Braunston, which was to be named the Birmingham & London Junction Canal. The proprietors were alarmed, especially as they had recently incurred vast expense in the construction of the new tunnel at Harecastle and the reservoir at Knypersley. They claimed that the principal landowners upon the proposed line, who included the Marquis of Hertford, the Earl of Cornwallis and the Earl of Craven, had declared publicly that they would oppose the scheme as 'unnecessary, and injurious to their property'. There was no need for this new canal, since Birmingham already had two canal links with London. The proprietors condemned the 'Speculative and excessive multiplication of Canals', and appealed to the public and the legislature for support.[41] Their opposition was successful, and the proposed canal was not built.

# 5
# Railway Competition

It is usually accepted that the railway era began in 1830 with the opening of the Liverpool & Manchester Railway, which was the first to carry passengers and goods by mechanical traction alone. The railways inevitably affected the prosperity of the canals, but in the case of the Trent & Mersey and Bridgewater Canals a long commercial life was still to come after 1830.

The first railway to threaten the Trent & Mersey was the Grand Junction, later part of the London & North Western Railway, which at first failed to obtain its act because of strong opposition from canal and coach proprietors and landowners. In 1833 the act was passed. The engineer was Joseph Locke and the line, which linked Birmingham with the Liverpool & Manchester Railway at Warrington, was opened in June 1837.[1] The Trent & Mersey's strong position had already been weakened by the opening of the Birmingham & Liverpool Junction Canal, which provided an alternative route to Liverpool for Staffordshire iron; and some canal customers were naturally ready to welcome competition in the interests of cheapness, convenience and speed. One such customer was an anonymous 'Manufacturer' who addressed the manufacturers of the Staffordshire Potteries in *Aris's Birmingham Gazette* in 1825:

> It should be observed that out of £74,580, £47,680 are lost to the Potteries, not from the regular charge of canal freight, but because our manufacture happens to be of a bulky description, and not adapted to the Canal Company's rule of 15 tons to each boat, a boat only being capable of receiving 7½ tons of earthenware, and because the Duke's Agents monopolize the carriage from Liverpool to Runcorn; and also from the necessity of carting all raw materials from the canal wharf to the various manufactories, averaging a mile of uphill draughts.

Short horse-drawn mineral lines existed in the Potteries. There was, for example, a line from the wharf on the Trent & Mersey Canal south of Whieldon's Grove to Longton, which was connected with some of the collieries by branch lines; this was still in use in the 1870s.[2]

The revenue of the Trent & Mersey in 1831 totalled £148,799; expenditure included £4,491 for the cost of additional locks in Cheshire, £3,208 for Parliamentary expenses, £97,500 for dividend payments, £15,234 for repairs to the navigation, and £651 for pensions and superannuated workmen.[3] In 1832, just before the authorisation of the Grand Junction Railway, the company announced that after 19 November of that year 'Rates, Tolls & Duties on most goods' would be reduced to 1d per ton per mile. The toll on coal and malt was to be reduced to $\frac{3}{4}$d per ton per mile, and that on paving stones to $\frac{1}{2}$d. These reductions did not apply to the Wardle branch of the Trent & Mersey.[4] This was only the first of a series of changes. In 1834 notice was given that after 17 May tonnage on ironstone would be reduced from 1d to $\frac{3}{4}$d per ton per mile, but in 1836 it was announced that from 12 November tonnage of 1d per ton per mile would be charged on 'Stone of every description'.[5] In 1836 an act was passed (1 Will IV c 55) to enable the company to acquire land to make double locks. They were also given authority to widen and straighten the Caldon branch between Oakmeadow lock and Flint Mill lock in order to improve the water supply to the mills and the navigation.

The estimated long-distance trade of the company in the year ending 30 June 1836 was 143,610 tons inwards and 184,500 tons outwards. The inward tonnage included 129,800 tons from Liverpool, largely clay and stone from Devon, Dorset and Cornwall (70,000 tons) and flintstone from Gravesend and Newhaven (30,000 tons); 8,260 tons from south Staffordshire, of which 7,000 tons were iron; 3,050 tons from London; and 2,500 tons from Manchester. The outward tonnage included 61,000 tons to Liverpool, of which 51,000 tons were earthenware and china; 59,500 tons to Manchester, of which 30,000 tons were bricks and tiles, and 25,000 tons were coal; 15,000 tons of limestone to south Staffordshire; 6,000 tons to Birmingham and the west of England; 42,000 tons to London, of which 12,000 tons were earthenware and china, and 30,000 tons were coal; and 1,000 tons of earthenware and china to Chester and North Wales. In addition there was a considerable local trade.[6]

At this time the Bridgewater trustees were hostile towards the Trent & Mersey, because the high tolls at Wardle Green prevented the joint reductions of toll which would have encouraged through traffic on the Middlewich branch. The high charge resulted in traffic from south Staffordshire and from the Welsh branch of the Ellesmere being diverted to Ellesmere Port. On 7 June 1838 Fereday Smith, the deputy superintendent of the Bridgewater trust, wrote to James Loch, the superintendent of the trust. Smith's letter describes the Trent & Mersey Canal Co as 'a set of persons who are not yet awake to their real interests, or who are unwilling to deviate from the course which was successfully (perhaps) pursued some years back when circumstances were in a different train to those under which all canal owners are now compelled to act, and who, moreover, are particularly sluggish in their motions'.[7]

Despite these criticisms, the Trent & Mersey Canal Co was gradually adopting a more realistic attitude and reductions continued to be made. On 2 May 1838 notice was given that gravel, stone and 'other road-making materials' would be carried at ½d per ton per mile from 5 June to 31 October 1838 and from 25 March to 31 October 1839. The toll on limestone was reduced to ½d per ton per mile on 11 May 1839, except on the Wardle branch; and on 24 June 1839 the toll on lime was also reduced to ½d per ton per mile. In the following year it was announced that after 1 June the rates of carriage for calcined and uncalcined iron-ore would be ¾d and ½d per ton per mile respectively. Further reductions followed: on 13 November 1840 the rates for linen, cotton, woollen and silk goods were reduced to ½d per ton per mile, except on the Wardle branch; on 15 January 1842 the toll on ale was reduced to ¾d per ton per mile, except on the Wardle branch; and on the same date the toll on road-making materials and manure was reduced to ½d per ton per mile 'at all times of the year'. On 4 July 1842 the toll for the carriage of timber, bricks and tiles on the Wardle branch was reduced to 6d per ton per 100yd; but this rate applied only if the boat had no other dutiable goods aboard. On 22 May 1843 the tolls on 'wrought iron, Slop Flint and Cornwall China Stone in the Slop State' were reduced to ½d per ton per mile.

On 14 August 1843 the toll on ale was raised to 1d per ton per mile, but the other reductions were maintained. On 19 August 1844 the toll on salt was reduced to ¾d per ton per mile, with the usual exception of the Wardle branch. On 25 January 1846 a reduced toll of ¾d per ton per mile was introduced for ale conveyed the 'whole distance between Horninglow or Shobnall and Shardlow, Fradley, Preston Brook'; and on the same date a reduced toll of ½d per ton per mile was introduced for all goods (except iron) conveyed 'the entire distance between Swarkestone and Fradley'.[8]

Railway competition could not be staved off indefinitely, and the dreaded 'Railroad Projectors' soon put forward three railway schemes which challenged the Trent & Mersey in the Churnet valley, in the Potteries, and in part of the Trent valley. In April 1845 the promoters of these schemes decided to act together, and in 1846 they sought authority to construct four lines. The first was to run from Macclesfield, the junction with the Macclesfield branch of the Manchester & Birmingham Railway, to Colwich, the junction with the Trent Valley Railway. The second was to run from Stone to Norton Bridge, the junction with the Grand Junction Railway. The third was to run from Harecastle to Crewe, the junction with the Grand Junction Railway. The fourth was to run from North Rode via Uttoxeter and Willington to Burton-on-Trent, the junction with the Birmingham & Derby Junction Railway. These projected railways, which were to become the North Staffordshire Railway, covered most of the area served by the canal. Faced with such a formidable challenge, the canal company decided that instead of opposing the bill they would seek to be taken over by the railway.

Favourable terms were negotiated for the canal shareholders, and on 12 July 1845 an agreement was signed between the railway promoters and the Trent & Mersey Canal Co. The selling price for the Trent & Mersey shares was set at their current price of £450. The current dividend was 30 per cent, and this was to be paid from the time of the passing of the bill to the opening of the whole line, when it was to be reduced to 22½ per cent. The railway lease was to date from 15 January 1847, and canal shares were then to be exchanged for 5 per cent railway preference shares. The profits thereafter were to be divided in proportion to the capital, until the canal shareholders had received a total of £30 per share.[9]

On 28 April 1846 James Sutton gave evidence in Parliament against the proposed amalgamation. Sutton was a canal carrier, and he believed that if the canal was taken over the railway company might close the locks in the evening in order to divert traffic from the canal to the railway. The canal company, he said, allowed boats to pass at all hours of the night, and they never let the water off for repairs for more than one week in the year. He pointed out that the company had authority to charge different rates to different places on the canal; and he said that because of competition from the Grand Junction, London & Birmingham and Midland Railways, they had in many cases reduced tolls by two-thirds. The general act of Parliament passed in June 1845 had enabled canal companies to vary tonnage rates in this way. The usual toll had been 1½d per ton per mile, but in most cases it had been reduced to ½d per ton per mile. Sutton paid tribute to the very low rates charged by the Trent & Mersey's carrying company, Hugh Henshall & Co; and he argued that if the amalgamation took place the railway proprietors might take over the whole of the carrying trade.

John Lewis Ricardo, chairman of the North Staffordshire Railway Co, also gave evidence on 28 April. Apart from the branch canal from Froghall to Uttoxeter, which the Trent & Mersey were already about to abandon because it was running at a loss of about £1,000 per annum, his company intended to keep the canal in repair and to work it. The Froghall–Uttoxeter branch was abandoned by the North Staffordshire Railway Act (10 & 11 Vict c 108) on 2 July 1847, and most of the canal bed was used for the Churnet Valley Railway in 1849, but traces of the canal exist at Oakamoor, Denstone and Rocester. Ricardo claimed to be promoting the North Staffordshire Railway entirely for the benefit of his constituents in the Potteries. For some time, he said, the Potteries had been almost the only large manufacturing district without the benefit of railway communication; and he attributed this fact to the opposition of the Trent & Mersey. The canal was no longer in a monopoly position, as was clearly shown by the reduction in tolls and by the reduction in the value of the shares from £1,200 to £450. Its favoured situation had been destroyed by competition from the Grand Junction Railway on one side and from the Midland Railway on the other.

Ricardo stated that the railway had been planned 'with a view to the traffic upon the canal'. The company had taken their line close to the canal wharfs, and had ensured that any railway branches that were needed could cross the canal without a special act. They intended to use the canal as a feeder, and would be able to take up goods on any part of the canal and bring them to the railway stations. Ricardo considered that canal tolls would almost certainly be lowered, because he believed nobody would send their goods by canal who could send them by the 'more expeditious means of a railway'. He undertook to promote goods traffic upon the canal, as goods traffic was 'rather an incumbrance than otherwise upon a railroad'. He believed, for this reason, that the canals would survive. Ricardo wanted to end the practice of charging higher tolls on goods coming by the Macclesfield Canal than upon those coming by the Bridgewater Canal.[10]

The act was passed on 26 June 1846, and on 23 September following the directors of the North Staffordshire Railway Co reported the transactions to their shareholders. They declared that the shareholders of the Trent & Mersey Canal Co were 'to a great extent, composed of influential landowners, Bankers, and Manufacturers on the Line, who had already successfully resisted several attempts to form a competing Line of Railway'; and they explained that they had judged it necessary 'to endeavour to effect some amicable arrangement with the powerful interests therein comprised'. The directors were optimistic about the prospects for the canal after the completion of the railway; they envisaged the canal and the railway as mutual feeders and believed that the profits on the canal might be augmented. They anticipated a saving of £300,000 in the cost of railway construction as a result of their ownership of the canal.

Three separate acts authorised the North Staffordshire Railway (9 & 10 Vic c 84, 85 and 86). By section 36 of 9 & 10 Vict c 84 the NSR undertook to maintain the canal's branches, railways, reservoirs, tunnels, towpaths, lands, buildings and works in good repair. The canal was to be kept 'dredged, cleaned and scoured, in good order and condition', except where parts of it were to be used 'for the purposes of the . . . North Staffordshire Railway'. The canal was valued at £1,170,000; on 13 July 1849, when the railway line had been completed, the capital was to be divided into 58,500 shares of £20 each. Three of the nine railway directors were obliged to become canal directors and hold their qualifica-

*Plate 13*   The Swan Inn at Fradley Junction *(Harry Arnold)*

*Plate 14*   The weir at Alrewas *(Harry Arnold)*

Plate 15   Wychnor Church *(Harry Arnold)*

Plate 16   The Malt Shovel Inn at Shardlow *(Harry Arnold)*

tions in canal shares. The NSR was authorised to raise capital to the amount of £2,900,000 and to borrow £965,000.[11]

On 1 July 1847, the report of the navigation committee announced a limitation of one month on carriers' credit. The committee stated that the proposed widening of the canal from the Potteries to Preston Brook, which had been approved by the Bridgewater trustees, was expected to cost £80,000, but that it had not been carried out because money was scarce. An arrangement had been made with the Staffordshire & Worcestershire Canal under which the tolls from Haywood to Preston Brook were to be ½d per ton per mile. Limestone was being sold to the south Staffordshire iron trade at its real value, and not as formerly at below cost price. A general tightening-up of discipline had taken place with the reintroduction of strict indexing and gauging of boats by day and by night. Traffic was to be allowed to pass at all hours. The wharf at Gainsborough was to be repaired and an agent installed there. A determined effort was to be made to recover the flour, malt and grain trade from Lincoln and Newark and the salt and timber trade between Hull and Liverpool. It was decided that the NSR should act as a canal carrier in an effort to persuade other carriers to reduce freight charges.[12]

The result of this decision was the North Staffordshire Railway & Canal Carrying Co, which established offices and a warehouse in Birmingham and agreed to act as carrying agents for the Worcester & Birmingham Canal.[13] On 18 July 1849 this carrying concern was taken over by the Bridgewater trustees who thereafter controlled most of Liverpool's trade with Manchester and Staffordshire. On 7 March 1853 James Loch's son George, who was one of the trustees, gave evidence against the proposed amalgamation of the NSR with the London & North Western Railway, which had taken over the Grand Junction, London & Birmingham, Trent Valley, and Manchester & Birmingham Railways. Loch explained that the trustees, fearing that the NSR might want to discourage canal trade through Preston Brook, had guaranteed to them an annual income of about £12,500 per annum, that being the amount the NSR had received in tolls during the previous year, on the understanding that they would 'make over to the Trustees the carrying trade into south Staffordshire, transferring to them their stations, and selling to them their boats, horses and their establishments and carrying stock at Wolver-

hampton'. George Loch said that the NSR had wanted to elimin-
ate the private carriers, but that 'four or five' of these carriers
were still operating.[14]

Robert J. Wilson has described some of the special features of
the boats which worked on the Trent & Mersey. The Anderton
Co's boats were known as 'Knobsticks'; the name is said to have
come either from the silver-tipped baton carried by the boat
marshal or from the fact that those who worked for the company
were so badly paid that they looked like knobsticks. At Middleport the company built its own boats, which carried about 20
tons. The most important cargo was crated earthenware goods,
the crates being either large barrels or large open-sided hampers.
A few of the crate-boats worked as fly-boats, and these had a crew
of four men instead of the usual two. The fly-boats usually
operated by night, and the extra speed was hard on the men and
the horses.[15] The *Directory of Staffordshire* for 1851 advertised fly-
boats from Stone to London and Manchester every night, and a
daily service of fly-boats to London, Manchester and Liverpool.
Pickfords, however, began to transfer their canal traffic to the
railways as early as 1838, and by 1841 had reduced the number of
their boats by 25 per cent.[16]

Trade at Shardlow declined in the 1840s because of competition
from the alternative route provided by the Cromford & High
Peak Railway, which linked the Cromford Canal to the Peak
Forest Canal. This route had been opened in 1831, but at first it
had not seriously competed for the cargoes from Nottinghamshire and Lincolnshire. These were transhipped at Shardlow
from the River Trent, carried on the Trent & Mersey to Preston
Brook, and conveyed from there to Manchester on the Bridgewater Canal. The situation was changed by the new railway lines,
such as the Manchester & Leeds Railway. In order to divert
traffic between Manchester and the Trent to their route via Selby,
the directors of the Manchester & Leeds reduced their rates. The
Trent & Mersey Co at first failed to respond to this challenge,
and carriers like Sutton and Soresby, who had previously sent
cargoes to Preston Brook, began to use the Cromford & High
Peak route. Tolls on the Trent & Mersey were then reduced;
but when the Shardlow premises of James Sutton & Co were
inspected on 5 October 1852, it was found that 'by the great
falling off of Traffic formerly passing through their hands the

occupation of the premises was very much reduced in value'. The rent for the next five years was therefore reduced from £250 to £125 per annum.[17]

Some glimpses of the canal workers' lives in the years following the amalgamation with the NSR are afforded by the minutes of the Trent & Mersey Navigation committee meetings at Stoke. On 19 October 1852 the canal superintendent recommended the enlarging of the crate sheds at Longport and Burslem and the provision of additional paving at the Burslem and Etruria wharfs. He also suggested that the company's carters should be provided during the winter season with oilskin coats at a cost of 8s each, and this proposal was accepted. On 25 January 1853 the owners of Severn boats working between Hayes Colliery and Haywood Junction were given permission to use donkeys to haul their boats on the canal. On 17 May 1853 £15 was granted for the relief of a destitute widow whose husband had been a tunnel-keeper at Preston Brook for nearly forty years, as the benefit society to which he had subscribed for nineteen years had failed. On the same date canal porters received increases in pay which raised the average rate to 18s a week. On 4 October 1853 it was announced that the wharfingers who occupied company houses were to pay an annual rent of £10, and that those who had hitherto paid no rent were to have this amount added to their salaries. On 1 November 1853, because of the increased prices of provisions and hay, the haulage rates for the company's boatmen were increased from 7d to 8d per mile; these rates were the allowances for the horses, which were owned by the boatmen.

On 29 November 1853 six new boats were ordered for the carrying trade between the Potteries and Liverpool, and on 13 December a tender of £150 per boat was accepted. The magistrates of Sandbach forbade the navigation of boats through their parish on Sunday, and this notice was laid on the table on 4 April 1854. Boatmen employed by the Bridgewater trustees, however, had navigated their boats on Sundays in the Cheshire district, and on 16 May 1854 it was reported that some of the men had appeared before the magistrates and had been fined 5s each for the offence. Attempts were made by the pottery agent of the trustees to remonstrate with the magistrates and stop further proceedings.

In the half-year ending 30 June 1854 the total receipts of the

carting department were £5,733; the expenditure was £4,323 and
the profits (exclusive of interest on capital) were £1,410. On 8
August 1854 attention was drawn to the state of the Burslem
basin, into which a 'noxious stream of sewage water was constantly running'. In 1853–4 there was an outbreak of cholera in
England, and the Burslem basin may have been the cause of some
cases. On 5 September 1854 it was reported that, because the
water-level in the reservoirs was low, boats working in opposite
directions were being required to wait for one another at the
locks to prevent wastage of water.

Salaries for canal clerks were increased in October 1854: that
of the booth clerk at Longport rose from £47 10s to £50, that of
the check clerk at Preston Brook from £30 to £35, and that of
the check clerk at Runcorn from £25 to £35. At the Stoke, Etruria
and Longport wharfs salaries rose from £150 to £160, £110 to
£120, and £100 to £110 respectively.[18]

In 1851 the NSR sought parliamentary authority for amalgamation with the London & North Western Railway. Charles
Mitchell, the agent for the Duke of Bridgewater's trustees at
Stockton Quay near Warrington, gave evidence against the
proposed amalgamation on 28 February 1853. He described the
extensive docks established at Runcorn by the late Duke and his
trustees, and the large warehouses which had been built at
Preston Brook and Runcorn for the traffic to and from the Trent
& Mersey Canal. He pointed out that the trustees had also provided docks, wharfage and warehouses for this traffic in Liverpool,
and that they had built warehouses for the Trent & Mersey carriers
in Manchester. About 1,000 tons per day passed between the
Bridgewater Canal and the Trent & Mersey at Preston Brook;
and the canals were used for the transit of manufactured goods,
cotton, hardware, sugar, tea, groceries, grain, timber, iron, slates,
china clay and earthenware. The LNWR was competing with
the canals for this traffic; if that company amalgamated with the
NSR, the directors might seek to discourage the carrying trade
on the Trent & Mersey in order to win more business for their
railway.

On 25 February 1853 William Matthews, the owner of collieries
and ironworks at Corbyn's Hall near Kingswinford in south
Staffordshire, gave evidence against the proposed amalgamation
of the two railways. He said that the Trent & Mersey Canal had,

in the hands of the NSR, served to a certain extent as a competing route to the north. Matthews feared that if the amalgamation took place the LNWR would be able to control all the traffic passing by water between Bristol and Lancashire, and that they might try to influence traffic going by the Staffordshire & Worcestershire Canal.[19] The Grand Junction Canal also opposed the bill: like the Bridgewater trustees they disliked the Trent & Mersey's high tolls, and they feared that the amalgamation would perpetuate these. Other canal companies which opposed the amalgamation were the Coventry Canal and the Leicestershire & Northamptonshire Union Canal. On 14 October 1854 the Leicestershire & Northamptonshire Union Canal turned down a proposal from the two railway companies, who were willing to sell or lease to them the Trent & Mersey Canal with its plant, wharfs, and warehouses, on condition that they withdrew their opposition to the amalgamation; they stated that the tolls on the Trent & Mersey were 'exorbitant', and that the offer to sell or lease the canal to them 'entirely overlooked' the interests of the public. On 18 October 1854 the Grand Junction Canal turned down the proposal on the same grounds; on 23 October 1854 the Coventry Canal gave the same reply, saying that they would continue their opposition to the amalgamation unless the tolls and dues were revised.[20] The bill for the proposed amalgamation was defeated.

After 1849, when the NSR was wholly opened, the revenue from the Trent & Mersey began to decline, but there was no comparable fall either in the tolls or in the profits. The figures for the years 1846–54 were as follows:[21]

| Year | Tonnage | Revenue (£) | Tolls (£) | Profits (£) |
|------|---------|-------------|-----------|-------------|
| 1846 | 1,339,965 | 136,450 | 109,948 | 71,027 |
| 1847 | 1,449,110 | 156,981 | 114,343 | 88,697 |
| 1848 | 1,361,622 | 173,771 | 98,665 | 73,945 |
| 1849 | 1,356,334 | 150,081 | 95,852 | 78,117 |
| 1850 | 1,258,984 | 121,428 | 87,402 | 69,425 |
| 1851 | 1,368,147 | 127,339 | 91,699 | 76,224 |
| 1852 | 1,308,157 | 118,639 | 85,430 | 69,383 |
| 1853 | 1,402,329 | 128,918 | 92,072 | 75,777 |
| 1854 | 1,385,833 | 133,587 | 93,117 | 76,126 |

On 17 April 1855 the Trent & Mersey Canal Co agreed to

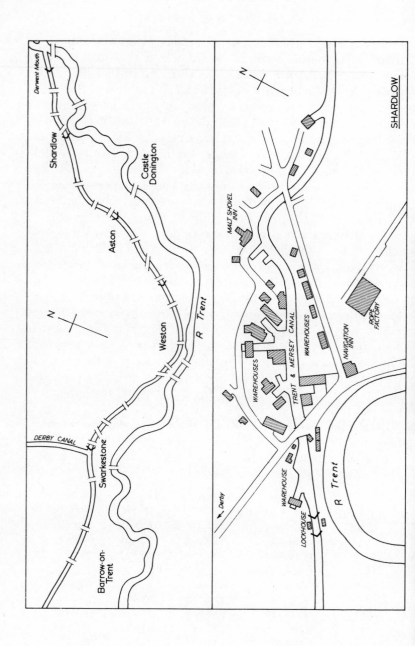

Derwent Mouth

Shardlow

Castle
Donington

Aston

Weston

R Trent

DERBY CANAL

Swarkestone

Barrow-on-
Trent

N

MALT SHOVEL
INN

WAREHOUSES

TRENT & MERSEY CANAL

WAREHOUSES

NAVIGATION
INN

ROPE
FACTORY

Derby

WAREHOUSE

LOCKHOUSE

R Trent

N

SHARDLOW

subscribe £100 towards the cost of a horse-bridge which the Trent Company had built across the River Trent near its junction with the Trent & Mersey at Derwent Mouth. On 26 June 1855 it was reported that Earl Granville had, without the company's permission, begun to erect a blacksmith's shop on land near his coal-pits. The Earl claimed that he was entitled to do this as lessee of the mines under the Duchy of Lancaster; but the company argued that as owners of the land they were entitled to compensation. On the same date the company turned down a request from the Rev. Eaton, who wanted to use one of their houses at Shardlow as a reading-room for his parish.

On 13 November 1855, the Burslem Gas Co gave an estimate of £31 for providing and laying down pipes and fittings for lighting the wharf, crate-sheds and office at the Burslem basin; this offer was accepted. At the same date, it was reported that the Bridge Road over the canal at Cauldon Place near Shelton was to be widened, and that the estimate for this was £60; the company agreed to contribute £20 towards the cost. On 11 December 1855 it was reported that navigation had been stopped for two days and three nights because of the accidental sinking of a loaded boat at the entrance to Trent lock at Alrewas, and orders were given that a set of screw-tackle for raising sunken boats should be provided for the use of the Fradley district.

The British Gas Light Co of London offered to pay an annual rent of £5 for a main through Harecastle tunnel and to supply the tunnel with gas at the rate of 5s per 1,000ft, but this offer was not accepted. The lack of lighting in the tunnels may perhaps have contributed to a fatal accident at Preston Brook; the coroner of Warrington, informing the company that a legger had fallen into the canal 'in a state of drunkenness', expressed the hope that the company would try to prevent such accidents.

On 1 April 1856 the company agreed to reduce from $\frac{3}{4}$d to $\frac{1}{2}$d per ton per mile the tolls upon coal carried by James Sutton & Co from their Trubshaw Colliery to Shardlow, but declined to give Sutton's fly-boats firm preference over the more heavily-laden boats in passing through the locks. On 27 May 1856 the toll on plaster stone conveyed from Swarkestone to Hall Green was reduced from $\frac{3}{4}$d to $\frac{1}{2}$d per ton per mile; and on 30 September 1856 the toll on cinders carried from Preston Brook to Haywood was reduced from $\frac{1}{2}$d to $\frac{1}{3}$d per ton per mile. On the same date

Thompson & Sons of Northwich were given permission to lay a brine feeder along the towpath at Marbury in return for an annual rent. On 28 October, at the request of the Marchay Colliery Co, the toll on coal from Willington to Fradley Junction was reduced from ¾d to ½d per ton per mile.

Burslem basin came in for more criticism on 25 November 1856 when complaints were made about bad service and inadequate accommodation. An inspection of the basin was arranged, and on 23 December 1856 it was stated that, in view of the large quantities of potters' material deposited on the wharf and the fact that all available space was occupied, the servants of the company were using 'all care that could reasonably be expected'. On the same date the toll on pig iron carried from Preston Brook to Etruria for the Shelton Bar Iron Co was reduced from 2s 11d to 2s 3d per ton.[22]

On 3 March 1857 a deputation from the Potteries Chamber of Commerce, accompanied by a solicitor, met the navigation committee to discuss the bill for the amalgamation of the Bridgewater Canal with the NSR. The Potteries Chamber of Commerce was against the bill, fearing monopoly control of transport to the Mersey. The proposal was for the railway to obtain a perpetual lease of the Bridgewater, Mersey & Irwell, Manchester & Salford Junction and Runcorn & Weston Canals, with their wharfs, docks and warehouses. A meeting of the iron-masters of Staffordshire to discuss the proposed amalgamation had agreed to oppose the bill. Later in the year the trustees of the Duke of Bridgewater stated that they were unable to provide accounts of the net earnings of the navigation. This created a problem, since the annual rent was to have been 90 per cent of the average profit for the previous three years. On 4 June 1857 the bill was abandoned.[23]

On 14 April 1857 it was proposed that tolls on earthenware should be reduced from 1½d to 1d, that tolls on clay, flints, china stone, chert stone, gypsum, plaster, bones and sand should be reduced from 1d to ⅔d, that tolls on coal should be reduced from ¾d to ½d, and that the toll of 10½d at Wardle lock and the extra toll on the part of the Macclesfield Canal belonging to the NSR should be abolished. These proposals were not accepted, as it was said that they would reduce by almost £9,000 the amount to be distributed among shareholders. In 1848 the canal had provided the pottery industry with transport for 58,287 tons of raw materials and 46,306 tons of earthenware. The tonnage figures for 1856 were much higher:

| Raw materials | 98,872 by canal; 11,068 by rail. |
|---|---|
| Earthenware | 63,376 by canal; 33,818 by rail. |

Distances on the canal were short, however, and the amount received in tolls in 1856 did not exceed £1,600.[24] The increase in tonnage was largely due to the expansion of trade in the Potteries. In 1778 Joseph Bramah had patented his water-closet, and the development and acceptance of his invention resulted in an important new branch of manufacture for the potters. In 1836 J. Buckley established his firm, which produced sanitary ware in Hanley; in 1849 Thomas Twyford, who came from a long line of potters, opened a factory in Bath Street, Hanley. In 1870 Thomas Twyford invented an improved all-earthenware water-closet, which was immediately successful. Other firms then entered the market: one of these was Doulton, who came from Lambeth in 1877 and took over potworks in Burslem. Sanitary ware was exported to France, Spain, Germany, Russia, the USA and Australia.

The population of Stoke-on-Trent rose steadily in the nineteenth century:[25]

| Year | Population |
|---|---|
| 1811 | 22,495 |
| 1821 | 29,223 |
| 1831 | 37,220 |
| 1841 | 47,951 |
| 1851 | 57,942 |
| 1861 | 71,308 |
| 1871 | 89,262 |
| 1881 | 104,968 |
| 1891 | 122,101 |
| 1901 | 140,335 |

Reductions in the toll upon slack sent from Preston Brook to Anderton were requested on 12 May 1857 by the salt proprietors at Anderton. This was a consequence of action by the Weaver trustees, who had reduced the toll to 4d a ton for the whole distance; the Trent & Mersey Canal Co charged 4½d per ton from Preston Brook to Anderton. The committee decided that a slight reduction might be made, provided that an increased amount of

the salt exported from Anderton was sent by canal instead of by
the Weaver. On 4 August the toll on rock salt carried from
Anderton to Preston Brook was reduced from ⅝d to ⅔d per ton
per mile; on 1 September the toll on coal carried from Preston
Brook to the salt works north of Hawdisher Lane in Wincham
was reduced from ⅝d to ½d per ton per mile. These reductions,
together with earlier reductions in the tolls on salt carried on the
Bridgewater Canal from Preston Brook to Runcorn, helped to
stimulate the trade in salt, coal, iron and manufactured goods
through the port of Runcorn, which was already the depot for
Staffordshire pottery.

In 1846 the quantity of salt exported from Runcorn was about
16,000 tons; in 1854 it had risen to 83,000 tons. By that date,
however, rail competition was diverting trade, and earthenware
was beginning to be sent to Birkenhead, where better facilities
existed. In 1852 a plan had been made for a canal from Runcorn
to the mouth of the Weaver at Weston Point. This had become
urgent in view of the possibility that the Weaver trustees might
build docks at Weston Point to enable salt to be transhipped there
instead of at Runcorn. This canal was eventually completed on
1 March 1860.

In the late 1850s quarrels broke out among the railway companies, and these were intensified by the slump in trade in the
autumn of 1857. Railway rates were cut, which made it more
difficult for the canals to compete. In October 1858 the LNWR
quarrelled with the NSR and began to carry out a survey for a
line into the Potteries from Whitmore or Madeley on what had
been the Grand Junction Railway. This would have taken traffic
away from Preston Brook. The potters would have welcomed a
new railway route into the Potteries from Birkenhead via Crewe,
since this would have allowed them to evade the heavy freight
charges on the NSR between Crewe and Stoke. The overthrow of
Captain Mark Huish, the general manager of the LNWR, helped
to bring about a reconciliation between the two railway companies, and in 1859 the two railways promoted another bill to
authorise their amalgamation; once again, however, this proposal
was defeated. In 1862 the high level of freight charges on the
Trent & Mersey was challenged by the potters, who claimed that
the NSR Co, as a railway and canal proprietor, was making their
raw materials unnecessarily expensive.[26]

Further plans for building railways into the Potteries were made in 1862. There were proposals for lines from Silverdale to Wellington and from Market Drayton, and there was a scheme for a canal from the Potteries to the Weaver capable of taking flats of 130 tons burden. In 1846 the NSR had been authorised to build a branch line from Stoke to Silverdale, and this threat had led the Newcastle-under-Lyme Junction Canal to abandon the Stubbs Walks part of their canal. In May 1851 the NSR agreed to purchase the section between Brampton Lane and Hassell Street for £1,000. Ralph Sneyd, the iron-master of Silverdale ironworks, had constructed a railway to carry coal and iron from his works to Pool Dam, half a mile from the Newcastle-under-Lyme Canal basin. By 1852 the NSR branch line to Newcastle-under-Lyme was in use; it joined the Silverdale & Newcastle-under-Lyme Railway at Knutton Junction. In 1856 a branch line to the Apedale Collieries was opened, and Sir Nigel Gresley's Canal became superfluous. About 1827 this canal had passed into the hands of Robert Edensor Heathcote, who was a shareholder in the Newcastle-under-Lyme Junction Canal and also a partner in the Apedale Collieries. In 1831 it had been suggested that Gresley's canal and the Junction Canal should be converted into railways, and George Stephenson had recommended that a steam-operated inclined plane be built to transfer boats between the two canals; but neither plan had been adopted. When Gresley's canal was defunct, Heathcote's wharf was moved to a siding between King Street and Hassell Street Bridge; the Junction Canal was sold for about £545 and finished its unsuccessful career in the spring of 1864.[27]

In 1853 the Newcastle-under-Lyme Canal had tried to fight off railway competition by building the Canal Extension Railway, a horse-drawn line, from their basin to Pool Dam and Sneyd's line. In 1859 Sneyd was authorised by the Silverdale & Newcastle-under-Lyme Railway Act to operate his line as a public one, and he obtained permission from the canal company to use their extension railway at the rate of 2d per ton. An act of 1860 allowed the NSR Co to lease the Silverdale & Newcastle-under-Lyme Railway; being thus hemmed in by the NSR, the Newcastle-under-Lyme Canal agreed in 1863 to lease their canal to the railway company. An undertaking was given that the canal would be kept in good repair and in working condition, and it was worked with the Trent & Mersey Canal. It had perhaps managed to 'assist the agriculture of the neighbourhood ... by a supply of lime at less expense', as the preamble to the act (35 Geo III c 37) had hoped, but it had never been profitable to its share-holders.

In 1921 an act was obtained which allowed the section from Newcastle-under-Lyme to Trent Vale to be filled in (NSR Act II and 12 Geo V c 117 local). The rest of the line was filled in to a point north of Church Street by 1938, when another act (LMSR 1 and 2 Geo VI c 27 local) allowed the canal to be filled in to its termination at Aqueduct Street. The only part of the canal which then remained was a short branch 100yd long; the main towpath and Copeland Street were still carried over this by the original bridges.[28]

The Macclesfield Canal, having turned down an offer from the NSR in October 1845, accepted in December an offer from the Sheffield, Ashton-under-Lyme & Manchester Railway; this involved a payment of £60,000 and a perpetual yearly rent of £6,605. The act (9 and 10 Vict c 266) was passed, and the Maccles-field and Peak Forest Canals were taken over by the railway company. The Macclesfield Canal's traffic continued to include coal, raw cotton, grain and stone; but it declined steadily, and by 1954 it was being used not for commercial traffic but for cruising.[29]

On 1 January 1863 the NSR responded to the threat of railway competition in the Potteries by reducing canal tolls on potters' raw materials. The Weaver trustees, who owned the Anderton carrying concern, reduced their charges by 10d per ton; at the same time they reduced their charges between Runcorn dock and Preston Brook from 2s 4d to 2s 2d per ton. Under an act of 1864, the NSR extended the line from Silverdale to Newcastle-under-Lyme to Madeley and Market Drayton.[30]

The Trent & Mersey Canal was clearly suffering from railway competition. In 1861 profits had been only £31,329, and in February 1862 the NSR report stated that 'while encouraging to the utmost the trade for which water-carriage is adapted, the Board have at the same time felt it incumbent upon them in no way to sacrifice for this purpose the resources of the Railway'. The 1866 minutes of evidence of the Royal Commission on Railways brought out clearly both the reduction in canal tolls and the transfer of traffic to the railway. The tolls on the Trent &

Mersey were reduced in January 1865 as follows: earthenware from 1½d to 1¼d per ton per mile, potters' materials from 1d to ¾d per ton per mile, pig iron from 1d to ¾d per ton per mile, and calcined ore from ¾d to ⅝d per ton per mile. Freight charges on earthenware going from the Potteries to Liverpool were reduced from 13s 6d to 12s 0d per ton; freight charges on potters' materials going from Liverpool to the Potteries were reduced from 7s 4d to 6s 9d per ton. It was asserted that the NSR got a greater revenue for earthenware carried between Liverpool and the Potteries out of the railway than out of the canal; and they intended 'as far as possible to develop the railway traffic rather than the canal'. The traffic carried on the railway was constantly increasing, as the following table shows:

| Year | Weight carried on canal in tons | Receipts from tolls (£) | Weight carried on railway in tons |
|------|---------------------------------|-------------------------|-----------------------------------|
| 1855 | 1,284,222 | 82,598 | 742,084 |
| 1856 | 1,537,882 | 102,366 | 897,185 |
| 1857 | 1,557,551 | 102,809 | 1,011,883 |
| 1858 | 1,363,384 | 85,508 | 941,323 |
| 1859 | 1,525,743 | 93,450 | 1,118,728 |
| 1860 | 1,595,217 | 98,776 | 1,244,786 |
| 1861 | 1,383,170 | 78,970 | 1,186,279 |
| 1862 | 1,555,333 | 88,910 | 1,267,270 |
| 1863 | 1,652,530 | 93,132 | 1,423,004 |

The total tonnage carried in 1849, before the full opening of the railway, was reported as 1,356,334; the total tonnage carried in 1863 was 3,075,534. The average receipt per ton on the canal in 1847, before any part of the railway was open, was 1s 7d; the average receipt per ton on the canal in 1863 was 1s 1½d.

P. Morris, speaking for the NSR, said that the LNWR had been granted running powers over the whole of their system, and that the NSR had running powers between Crewe and Liverpool, between Macclesfield and Manchester, and between Norton Bridge and Birmingham. The LNWR exercised their running powers through the Potteries and the mineral district, but not through the purely agricultural districts. The number of workers in the pottery trade had been increasing: in 1851 25,022 people had been employed, whereas in 1861 the figure was 27,432.[31] There was prosperity in the Potteries, and a great increase in trade had followed the arrival of the railways.

The canal charged reduced tolls on most goods from 1 March 1866. The gross toll upon all goods passing off or on at Hall Green or Wardle lock was not to exceed the gross toll on the same goods passing over the same ground to or from Preston Brook. The toll at Wardle lock, however, remained at 9d per ton per mile on coal, coke, culm, limestone and rock salt, at 9½d on timber, free-stone, slates, ironstone, lead ore, iron and lead, and at 10½d on all goods and merchandise. The excessive tolls at Wardle and at Hall Green were finally reduced by the Railway and Canal Traffic Act of 1888.

# 6
# Commercial Decline

By the 1860s better relations had been established between the North Staffordshire Railway and London & North Western Railway companies, and this had brought to an end the rate-cutting wars which had proved so ruinous to canal traffic. In the 1870s, however, a new threat to traffic on the Trent & Mersey was posed, not by the railways but by the Weaver trustees, who were improving facilities at Anderton and were doing all they could to divert traffic to their route. In 1866 they had obtained an act which had resulted in the deepening of the river and the improvement of the locks, and in 1870 meetings to discuss the threatening situation were held by a canal traffic committee consisting of representatives of the Bridgewater trustees, the Shropshire Union Railways & Canal Co (which had taken over the Ellesmere & Chester and Birmingham & Liverpool Junction Canals) and the NSR Co. This committee met at intervals in the years 1867–75, mainly to fix freight charges between north Staffordshire and Liverpool. On 9 November 1867 the NSR Co agreed to reduce by 6d per ton the rates for potters' materials between the Mersey and the Potteries.[1] It was agreed on 29 April 1870 that rates of 3d and 2d per ton would be charged on white salt and rock salt respectively, provided a minimum quantity of 135,000 tons of white salt and 55,000 tons of rock salt were sent annually along the Trent & Mersey Canal via Preston Brook for shipment on the Mersey; these quantities could be varied, provided the gross toll payable to the NSR Co amounted to the sum of £2,145 per annum. Freight charges from Liverpool to the following places were also agreed:

|  | Potters' materials | | Flints and cherts | |
|---|---|---|---|---|
|  | s | d | s | d |
| Tunstall | 5 | 9 | 5 | 4 |

| Longport and Burslem | 5 | 11 | 5 | 5 |
|---|---|---|---|---|
| Etruria | 6 | 2 | 5 | 7 |
| Stoke | 6 | 5 | 5 | 9 |

The Bridgewater trustees allowed the NSR a further discount of 2d per ton on all potters' materials carried by the NSR, and the NSR agreed to allow a discount of 1½d per ton on all potters' materials carried by the Anderton Co from Preston Brook.

On 10 May 1870 it was reported that the Weaver trustees were taking further action to divert traffic to their route, and that this included reductions in their rates: the Trent & Mersey Canal Co therefore agreed to reductions on potters' raw materials to the extent of 6s per ton. On 26 July news was received that the ironmasters had guaranteed not less than 16,000 tons of iron per annum for two years to the Weaver route, on the understanding that the rate should be about 6d per ton less than that then charged by the Preston Brook and Ellesmere Port routes. In view of this, the NSR agreed to reduce rates on iron by 6d per ton. On 19 August the NSR decided to charge the full Parliamentary toll on traffic interchanged at Anderton.

On 13 March 1871 the prospectus of the proposed Traders (North Staffordshire) Carrying Co Ltd was examined and approved by the chairman of the Potteries Chamber of Commerce and by Godfrey Wedgwood. The aim was to carry raw materials and manufactured goods between the River Mersey and north Staffordshire via Weston Point, the River Weaver and Anderton. The NSR tried to compete by reducing their rates on iron, but on 22 January 1872 it was reported that the Weaver trustees were planning to link their waterway with the Potteries on a much larger scale. For the 1872 session they prepared a bill to authorise a new connection from the Anderton basin to the Trent & Mersey, which would permit the interchange of cargoes in boats between the Weaver Navigation and the canal. The main elements of the scheme were the following:

1 a cut from the eastern side of the western arm of the Anderton basin;

2 an aqueduct which would carry this cut across the north-eastern part of the Anderton basin;

3 a side-dock at the end of this aqueduct, between the north-eastern side of the basin and the canal;

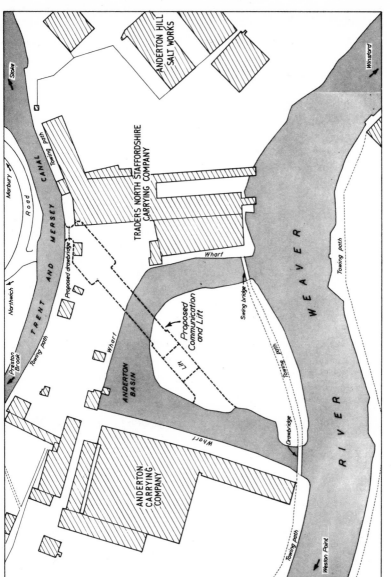

9 Anderton in 1872

4 a cut from this side-dock through the towpath and into the canal;

5 'all necessary basins, stop-gates, lifts, inclines, sluices, bridges, aqueducts and culverts for the purpose of the said communication.'

The bill was to enable the trustees to make compulsory purchase of land and houses, and to divert water from the Weaver and from the Trent & Mersey Canal for the side-dock and cut. It was also to authorise the trustees and the NSR Co to enter into agreements about the working of the proposed connection and the fixing and levying of tolls in respect of the interchange traffic. The preamble to the bill described the existing arrangement at Anderton as costly and slow. The interchange area contained steam-hoist machinery, a goods tramway, a rock-salt incline tramway, a shed for the rock-salt wagons, a shed for the workmen, a pigsty, a smithy, a stable, a calf-shed, an engine-house, a drawbridge, offices and store rooms.

In place of the arrangement whereby goods were interchanged by means of these hoists, tramways, shoots and inclines, the act authorised the construction of a lift. The lift, designed by the engineer of the Weaver trustees, E. Leader Williams, had a huge iron framework which contained a pair of water-filled tanks of wrought iron, with watertight guillotine gates at each end. Each tank could accommodate two narrow boats or one barge from the Bridgewater Canal. A wrought-iron aqueduct 162ft 6in long, with three arches, connected the upper level of the lift with the canal via a small side-lock.[2] Originally the lift was worked by hydraulic power: a steam-engine supplied a hydraulic accumulator, which allowed the downward movement of one caisson while the other travelled up to the higher level. If one tank was under repair, the other could operate independently. The actual lifting took seven minutes.

The lift cost about £48,000 and was opened in 1875. Transhipment of salt from canal boats to river barges continued by means of chutes alongside the lift. After an accident in 1882, when one of the presses burst and a caisson containing a boat fell 5oft, some modifications were made. A charge of 1s per boat plus 1d per ton was allowed, but in 1886 the lift was free to those who had paid tolls on the River Weaver.[3] In 1903 electricity replaced

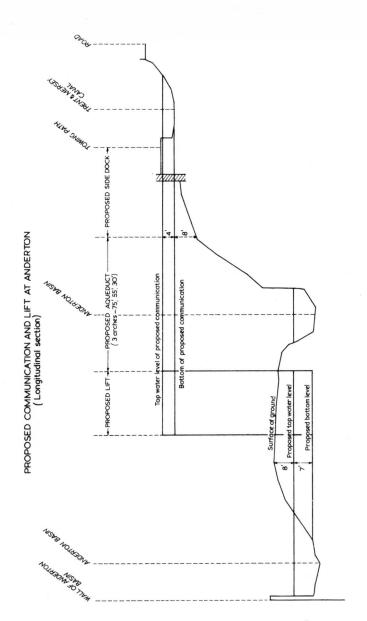

PROPOSED COMMUNICATION AND LIFT AT ANDERTON
( Longitudinal section )

ROAD

TRENT & MERSEY CANAL

TOWING PATH

PROPOSED SIDE DOCK

PROPOSED AQUEDUCT
(3 arches — 75', 55', 30')

ANDERTON BASIN

PROPOSED LIFT

Top water level of proposed communication

Bottom of proposed communication

4'

8'

Surface of ground

8'

Proposed top water level

7'

Proposed bottom level

ANDERTON BASIN

WALL OF ANDERTON BASIN

10  Plan for the Anderton lift

steam, and by 1908 the hydraulic system had been replaced by counterbalance weights.

Tonnage and tolls for the Trent & Mersey Canal for the years 1864 to 1873 were as follows:

| Year | Tonnage | Tolls (£) | Profits (£) |
|------|---------|-----------|-------------|
| 1864 | 1,594,028 | 88,463 | 69,428 |
| 1865 | 1,476,283 | 75,985 | 56,172 |
| 1866 | 1,553,166 | 82,815 | 65,945 |
| 1867 | 1,510,238 | 78,686 | 59,774 |
| 1868 | 1,494,524 | 71,595 | |
| 1869 | 1,549,506 | 74,600 | |
| 1870 | 1,562,786 | 73,089 | |
| 1871 | 1,481,122 | 71,234 | |
| 1872 | 1,439,390 | 71,690 | |
| 1873 | 1,337,802 | 67,108 | |

During these years the decline in traffic was gradual.

In 1872 the Staffordshire Potteries Chamber of Commerce voiced its opposition to a new proposal for the amalgamation of the NSR and the LNWR. They argued that such an amalgamation would remove the fear of rival lines, and that this would result in reduced facilities for the carriage of goods and passengers. Staffordshire had already suffered from the lack of competition between railways and canals, but the situation would become worse if the LNWR took over both, as they would not have the same interest as the NSR in keeping open the canal and would force as much traffic as possible on to the railway. The Potteries Chamber of Commerce concluded by saying that some of the most important manufactories and mills had been built beside the canal, and that water carriage was essential to the Potteries. On 2 May 1872, J. Allport, the traffic manager of the Midland Railway, gave evidence to the Select Committee on Railway Companies Amalgamation. He said that the Trent & Mersey had 99 per cent of the traffic in china clay from Runcorn to the Potteries, and that there was a return trade in salt via Runcorn to Cornwall. He suggested that the canals might be taken over by the state, in order that canal traders might be encouraged to maintain independent competition with the railway companies. Allport doubted, however, whether this competition could be maintained except for short distances and special traffic.[4] In this same year the Bond End Canal, which linked the Trent & Mersey with the River Trent at Burton, fell into disuse.

Both tonnage and tolls declined in 1874, and a statement in the NSR minutes reported that the canal had been unfavourably affected by the declining trade in potters' raw materials and in earthenware. The increasing transference of traffic to the railway had augmented the railway revenue, but not sufficiently to compensate for the tolls lost by the diminished trade on the canal.[5] On 1 February 1875 it was reported that the tolls had declined so far that they no longer met the guaranteed dividends. The directors were examining the matter with 'anxious consideration'.

From 1874 to 1879 there was little improvement in the figures for tonnages and tolls:

| Year | Tonnage | Tolls (£) |
|------|---------|-----------|
| 1874 | 1,187,047 | 57,504 |
| 1875 | 1,189,407 | 57,490 |
| 1876 | 1,096,060 | 52,155 |
| 1877 | 1,142,975 | 53,760 |
| 1878 | 1,084,260 | 50,520 |
| 1879 | 1,043,582 | 48,751 |

In 1880, however, the tonnage rose to 1,244,318, and the income from tolls to £61,410.

In the same year the NSR proposed a bill, promoted by the owners of the Caldon quarries, which sought to alter the course of their railway lines. In 1849 the NSR had built their fourth and last railway, which replaced the 1802 tramroad. It was cable-operated and of 3ft 6in gauge, and had four self-acting planes. Each train was composed of up to nine wagons carrying 6 tons each, and up to 1,000 tons of limestone a day were transported. Much of the limestone went by canal to the works of Brunner Mond in Northwich, which was later taken over by ICI. At Upper Cotton there was a tunnel about 60 chains long. On 8 February 1884 it was reported that the line of rails at Caldon had been extended nearer to the face of the quarry. Quarrymen from North Wales came to Caldon Low, and a large Welsh population settled there.[6]

In August 1884 a bill to authorise a Manchester Ship Canal was opposed by the NSR, as it seemed to threaten their canal interests.

This bill failed early in 1885, but a similar one was passed in August of the same year. Other ship canal projects, which were put forward without success, included a Birmingham & Liverpool Ship Canal. This was to run from the River Weaver at Winsford via the Potteries and Stafford to Wolverhampton and Birmingham; and for a time the NSR considered modernising and improving the Trent & Mersey, so that it could become part of the scheme. On 5 February 1886 it was announced that maintenance of the canal was to be separated from that of the railway, and a canal engineer was appointed. Dredging of the canal began and by 1906 'over 1,100,000 cubic yards of earth had been dredged up'; the width and depth of the canal between the Potteries and Runcorn was so much increased that the barges could carry 28 tons between these points, compared with 21 tons in 1886.

In February 1887 notice was given of a bill to improve the Trent Navigation and widen the Trent & Mersey Canal from Shardlow to Burton; this was passed in August. The traffic for the years 1881 to 1891 was as follows:

| Year | Tonnage | Tolls (£) |
| --- | --- | --- |
| 1881 | 1,202,568 | 58,305 |
| 1882 | 1,244,128 | 60,552 |
| 1883 | 1,240,121 | 58,756 |
| 1884 | 1,204,999 | 55,328 |
| 1885 | 1,160,607 | 53,415 |
| 1886 | 1,088,605 | 50,560 |
| 1887 | 1,115,893 | 51,841 |
| 1888 | 1,139,098 | 53,455 |
| 1889 | 1,116,445 | 53,689 |
| 1890 | 1,075,547 | 50,531 |
| 1891 | 1,052,758 | 49,533 |

An act obtained in 1891 (54 and 55 Vict c 34) authorised the widening and straightening of the Trent & Mersey between Stoke-on-Trent and Preston Brook. The towpath in the Harecastle tunnel was to be removed, although this was not carried out until much later, and the NSR Co was to provide steam tugs for compulsory towage through the tunnel. The thirty-five locks between Stoke and Preston Brook were to be replaced by twenty-one larger ones, each 135ft by 15ft by 6ft, which could accommodate a steam barge carrying 40 tons and towing a butty of 50 to 80 tons burden. There was opposition to the bill from traders who feared that it was intended only as a means of preventing the construction of the Birmingham & Liverpool Ship Canal. W. Douglas Phillipps, the general manager of the NSR, denied these accusations. Giving evidence in 1906, however, he stated that the company had carried out the work for duplicating the locks at the north end of the new Harecastle tunnel, where there was 'a little bit of a bottleneck', but that apart from the dredging work no other improvements had been made. Phillipps said that the number of barges passing through the summit lock at Harecastle was between 170 and 180 a day, which was more than could be got through a single lock without serious delay.

The Railway and Traffic Act of 1888 set up the Railway and Canal Commission on a permanent basis in place of the Railway Commission, and allowed the Board of Trade to establish a uniform classification of merchandise to be applied to all railways. After eighty-five days of discussion in 1889 and 1890, when the special commissioners appointed by the Board of Trade heard the companies' proposals and objections, the new maximum rates were authorised by a series of Railway (Rates and Charges) Order Confirmation Acts in 1891 and 1892. Parliament passed the Railway and Canal Traffic Act in 1894, and thereafter the railway companies had to justify any increase in rates before a court if a trader made a complaint about it to the Railway and Canal Commission. This in turn meant that the railway companies could not raise rates easily; they were therefore reluctant to lower them.

On 10 August 1894 the consequences of the Railway and Canal Traffic Act of 1888 were described by the NSR. The legal expenses incurred in the course of the inquiries held before a Joint Parliamentary Committee, and before the authorities representing the Board of Trade, had amounted with respect to the canal alone to nearly £500. Much time and labour had also been lost, and the new schedule of tolls would result in 'a serious diminution of the receipts of the Canal'. The canal's income was said to be already insufficient to meet the 5 per cent interest guaranteed on the preferential shares to the canal proprietors. Under these circumstances it was considered necessary to stop 'for the time being' the improvements that had been contemplated. The work to be undertaken would now be limited to the 'maintenance of a sufficient waterway and to the most simple and

essential repairs'. The enlargement of the canal between Anderton
and Middlewich had been carried out in 1891 at a cost of £22,000,
and this meant that barges carrying 60 tons could travel from the
Mersey as far as Middlewich. When the Croxton aqueduct was
built, however, this section was narrowed; the aqueduct is now a
steel structure only 8ft 2in wide.[7] In 1895 the NSR Co's carrying
trade was discontinued.

Revenue was £80,175 in 1888, but had fallen to £54,180 in
1898. Tonnages and tolls for the years 1892 to 1902 were as
follows:

| Year | Tonnage | Tolls (£) |
|------|---------|-----------|
| 1892 | 1,073,116 | 50,474 |
| 1893 | 1,012,950 | 48,823 |
| 1894 | 1,052,567 | 49,647 |
| 1895 | 1,098,058 | 45,207 |
| 1896 | 1,248,219 | 51,131 |
| 1897 | 1,209,539 | 48,822 |
| 1898 | 1,215,540 | 48,866 |
| 1899 | 1,212,093 | 49,072 |
| 1900 | 1,168,430 | 47,472 |
| 1901 | 1,146,087 | 46,773 |
| 1902 | 1,131,581 | 46,294 |

In 1894 an act was obtained for enlarging Rudyard Reservoir,
and 8ft was added to its height. The Manchester Ship Canal,
which opened in 1894, proved a commercial success. In the same
year the NSR Co promoted a bill to enable them to provide
haulage of boats through the Harecastle tunnel with tugs worked
electrically or by means other than steam, and to make a charge
for the service. The North Staffordshire Chamber of Commerce
and other traders opposed this clause, because it would mean
that they would be compelled to use the tugs and be unable to
use their own horses or leggers. The authorisation was given, but
an electric tug was not in operation until 30 November 1914.

The electric tug was a steel barge which had two 15 hp motors
driving winches, and these winches pulled the vessel along by
means of a wire rope which was fastened at each end of the
tunnel. Power was provided by a second boat with about 100
batteries in it, which transferred the power to the first tug. There
was a generating station on the island at the mouth of the tunnel,
and one boat charged its batteries while the other one was

working. About 1920 a trolley overhead wire was laid on the
tunnel roof, and this made the batteries unnecessary. A charge of
6d per boat was made, and the tug remained in use until 1954,
when self-propelled boats began to use the tunnel and ventilating
equipment was installed at the south end.

Tunnel steam-tugs had been introduced at Preston Brook at
the beginning of 1865, but ventilation was lacking at first so that,
as Peter Norton has described, one tug driver and his stoker were
overcome by the fumes of the coal fire. To remedy the situation
Mr Forbes, the resident engineer of the canal, ordered four
ventilating shafts to be sunk at Preston Brook. One of the two
maintenance men working in the shafts inside the tunnel was
drowned when he was overcome by the fumes in May 1865, and
at the inquest on 27 May the jury recommended that the NSR Co
should discontinue the use of the tug boat until the four air
shafts were completed. The maintenance men had hitched a lift
in an ice-boat by fixing it on to the end of a train of boats,
unknown to the tug driver, and it was recommended that this
practice should be discontinued. Steam-tugs were used in the
Barnton and Saltersford tunnels also.

In 1906 a report on the state of the Trent & Mersey Canal was
given in the *Minutes of Evidence of the Royal Commission on the
Canals and Inland Navigations of the United Kingdom*. Giving evidence
on 22 May W. Douglas Phillipps referred to the reduction in
tolls which had taken place in 1846, 1865, 1868 and 1892. He
claimed that there was 'always a kind of prejudice in favour of the
canal as against the railway', and argued that this was because the
canal extended beyond the NSR at each end. He said that there
were several potworks on the canal, and that they found the canal
cheaper to use than the railway. One reason for the decline in
traffic was that the ironworks in south Staffordshire no longer
sent their products via the canal and the Trent Navigation to
Hull, for export to Germany. This was partly because of competition from the Midland Railway, and partly because of the
poor state of the Trent navigation. Phillipps said that the Harecastle tunnels could not be increased in size, and that they could
be avoided only by 'a lift or other device'.

The canal carriers mentioned in the evidence included Fellows,
Morton & Co, a 'most esteemed customer'; the Anderton Co,
'very large carriers', organised by the Bridgewater trustees until

1876; Brunner Mond & Co, who had a large fleet of boats plying regularly between the quarries at Froghall and their works at Sandbach; and the Salt Union, whose large fleet of boats carried salt from the factories at Middlewich to Anderton. Phillipps claimed that the Trent & Mersey was in better order than any other canal in Great Britain, but he had to agree that the narrow boats which operated between Middlewich and Burton were not capable of carrying heavy traffic in competition with the railway. He said that 50,000 or 60,000 tons of pottery a year were taken down to Runcorn in narrow boats, transhipped there into floats or lighters, and then taken across the Mersey to the various Liverpool docks. China clay was brought from Cornwall and Dorset, and attempts by the Great Western Railway and the South Western Co to take over the canal's traffic in clay had failed. The canal also carried a large coal traffic for short distances. In the year 1905 the interchange traffic had been as follows:

| Point of transhipment | Other navigation | Tonnage to the T & M | Tonnage from the T & M |
|---|---|---|---|
| Derwent Mouth | Trent | 8,866 | 10,417 |
| Swarkestone | Derby Canal | 3,585 | 3,258 |
| Fradley | Coventry Canal | 2,499 | 10,179 |
| Great Haywood | Staff & Worcs | 18,945 | 28,478 |
| Hall Green | Macclesfield | 657 | 15,152 |
| Wardle lock | Shropshire Union | 6,623 | 8,517 |
| Anderton | Weaver | 25,372 | 764 |
| Preston Brook | Bridgewater Canal | 41,917 | 31,699 |
| | | 108,464 | 108,464 |

German import duties had almost entirely killed the traffic in earthenware from the Potteries to Hull, and this was accepted as irreversible. The canal was not used for agricultural traffic at all. The three large classes of traffic were coal and limestone (lowest class), clay and other pottery materials (middle class), and manufactured earthenware (highest class). The competition among carriers was said to be very keen, and there was some undercutting. The central section of the canal was too narrow to be used by the larger boats. The cost of maintaining the canal for one year was £25,625, and 73 per cent of the gross receipts were spent on the upkeep of the canal. The NSR lost money on the canal because the profits did not meet the interest which the railway company had to pay on the original capital. Fred Morton, a director of Fellows, Morton & Clayton Ltd, praised the NSR for their treatment of carriers. He said that a boat would carry 25 tons of flints or china clay, but only 8 tons of earthenware. The cost of haulage was five times higher on the canals than on the railways, but the canal carriers could transport goods for 10 per cent less than the railway companies, because the railway companies had to pay heavily to maintain their permanent way.[8]

The evidence given to the royal commission brought out the disadvantages of the canal as well as its advantages. The changes in width hindered through-traffic; and the locks, bridges and tunnels slowed down all traffic. The railways could take smaller loads, thus avoiding the delays caused by the need to wait for a full boat-load. Heavy materials such as coal and clay, however, continued to be carried by water, and the Potteries still depended on the canal.

Tonnages and tolls from 1903 to 1912 were as follows:

| Year | Tonnage | Tolls (£) |
|------|---------|-----------|
| 1903 | 1,195,756 | 48,878 |
| 1904 | 1,193,444 | 49,815 |
| 1905 | 1,137,663 | 50,273 |
| 1906 | 1,130,426 | 51,295 |
| 1907 | 1,134,829 | 52,400 |
| 1908 | 1,007,008 | 46,543 |
| 1909 | 1,017,371 | 47,834 |
| 1910 | 1,065,424 | 50,595 |
| 1912 | 1,059,035 | |

Proposals for the improvement of the canal system were put forward in the report of the royal commission in 1910. These included the amalgamation and enlargement of the canals on the four main routes which joined in Staffordshire. The route from Fradley Junction via Burton-on-Trent to Nottingham and the Humber should be improved to 300-ton standard between Fradley and Nottingham and to 750-ton standard from Nottingham to the Humber. The route from Birmingham and Wolverhampton to the Mersey should include canals of 100-ton standard from Aldersley Junction northwards, and also from Birmingham via the Coventry and the Trent & Mersey.[9] The canals themselves had little capital, and these proposals would have required very large public expenditure. They were never put into effect, and the commissioners' efforts to improve the canal system failed.

The quarries at Caldon Low, which had produced between 65,000 and 100,000 tons of limestone per annum in the years 1825–30, faced competition in the 1840s from the Black Country producers and from South Wales; and by 1851 the Clay Cross Co was successfully selling Derbyshire limestone in south Staffordshire. The Caldon Low quarries managed to compete, and after about 1865 they entered a period of prosperity. By the early years of the twentieth century, however, the original quarries were worked out and abandoned.

In 1905 a standard gauge branch railway, 61 chains long, was opened from the NSR Leek–Waterhouses line at Caldon Junction to serve the new quarries further east near Waterhouses. Competition from the railway became severe, and there was a large decrease in canal traffic. The Brunner Mond works at Sandbach, which had been one of the chief customers for limestone, closed down in 1920. On 25 March of the same year there was a slip on the canal at the Froghall basin, and the cable-line between Froghall and the Caldon quarries was closed. The track was lifted on the incline in 1921, and in 1923 the Caldon quarries were acquired by the London Midland & Scottish Railway, which leased them in 1934 to Hadfields of Sheffield.[10]

After the outbreak of World War I, the Trent & Mersey Canal was controlled by the government through the Railway Executive Committee. Canal staff were called up and tonnage declined steadily. In 1918 there was some ministerial support for the public ownership of transport, and in March David Lloyd George told a deputation from the TUC that he was in 'very, very complete sympathy' with their demand for the nationalisation of railways and inland waterways. In December 1918 Winston Churchill informed the Dundee Chamber of Commerce that the government intended to nationalise the railways. Sir Eric Geddes was given the task of preparing a bill which would allow the Ministry of Ways and Communications to increase its control over railways, light railways, roads, canals, docks, harbours and shipping, electric power, tramways and other road vehicles.

Opposition to these proposals was strong and the Federation of British Industries voiced its hostility. In the Commons the bill was so much altered that when it passed its third reading it bore little relation to the original proposal of overall government control. On 15 August the bill became law, and Sir Eric Geddes became the first British Minister of Transport. He told the Commons on 24 June 1920 that the Cabinet had decided against nationalisation of the railways. On 19 August 1921 four regional groupings of railways were established: Southern, Great Western, London & North Eastern, and London, Midland & Scottish.[11] The Trent & Mersey Canal came under the control of the London, Midland & Scottish Railway. Tonnages had fallen sharply, and continued to decline:

| Year | Tonnage |
|------|---------|
| 1924 | 534,821 |
| 1930 | 423,276 |
| 1933 | 318,086 |
| 1934 | 300,735 |
| 1935 | 323,733 |
| 1936 | 319,080 |
| 1937 | 310,153 |
| 1938 | 385,870 |

One of the reasons for this fall was the decline of south Staffordshire as a producer of coal and iron. The number of blast furnaces had steadily diminished from the early 1880s, and collieries and ironworks had closed down. The railway continued to compete with the Trent & Mersey for through traffic, and improved road transport competed with the canal for short-distance traffic. Coal freight was also affected by new competing fuels such as oil.

From the mid-1890s the boatmen's standard of living seems to have declined, and there was increased pressure for wives to make their homes on the boat. Family boatmen were more prosperous, although education of the children often proved impossible. The introduction of motor boats was not general on the Trent & Mersey until World War II, but Fellows, Morton & Clayton operated steamers from about 1880. These steamers were narrow boats with elm bottoms and iron sides. Before World War I, Fellows, Morton & Clayton had begun to replace the steamers with narrow boats whose semi-diesel engines occupied less space than the steam boiler and engine. The Anderton Co introduced its first motor boat in 1924.[12]

On the outbreak of World War II, those canals which were

controlled or owned by railway companies came once again under
the authority of the Railway Executive Committee. In June 1940,
to compensate for the lost trade in imports passing from east-
coast to west-coast ports, the government gave canal carriers a
subsidy equal to 50 per cent of tolls. In 1942 eighteen canal
companies and forty-two carriers were brought under the control
of the Ministry of War Transport. The aim was to use the canal
network more fully, but the ministry found it difficult to adjust
the canals to the demands of war. The canals had been neglected
during the inter-war years, and in the first two years of the war
they had lost many of their boatmen to war service. Tonnages
for the years 1940 to 1945 were as follows:

| Year | Tonnage |
|------|---------|
| 1940 | 237,981 |
| 1941 | 223,468 |
| 1942 | 225,950 |
| 1943 | 240,056 |
| 1944 | 237,309 |
| 1945 | 198,136 |

The canals were allowed to run down during the war, because
the differing gauges made it impossible to work them efficiently
as a coordinated system of through traffic. In 1947 the Transport
Act was passed and the canals, almost without discussion, came
into public ownership. The Trent & Mersey, like most British
canals, was taken over on 1 January 1948 by the British Transport
Commission.

By the London, Midland & Scottish Act of 1944 the Leek
branch had been abandoned as 'unnecessary'. The coal trade
from Foxley to Leek had ended in 1934, and after 1939 there was
no trade in tar from Leek to Milton, so the line was no longer
used. After World War II the Caldon Canal lost its traffic in clay
to Stanley and in felspar to Milton; and after 1951, when it
ceased to transport coal from Park Lane to Brittain's Paper Mills
at Cheddleton, it no longer had any commercial traffic.[13]

Tonnages from 1946 to 1956 were as follows:

| | |
|------|---------|
| 1946 | 186,020 |
| 1947 | 155,866 |
| 1949 | 130,280 |
| 1950 | 142,591 |

| | |
|---|---|
| 1951 | 135,189 |
| 1952 | 132,738 |
| 1953 | 89,183 |
| 1954 | 106,219 |
| 1955 | 85,740 |
| 1956 | 90,326 |

In 1955 the report of the Board of Survey on Canals and Inland Waterways was published. This showed that the decline in traffic on the Staffordshire canals had continued. The National Coal Board had closed some loading basins, which had led to a fall in the quantity of domestic and industrial coal conveyed by canal. The Board of Survey reported that major improvements, such as the widening of the locks and the strengthening of the banks, were essential if the narrow canals were to be able to carry larger and faster boats capable of competing with other forms of transport. The Trent & Mersey Canal was included in the list of waterways which were to be maintained to an adequate standard of efficiency.[14] In 1956 the north-western division of British Transport Waterways was reorganised; canals south of the Mersey were to be controlled by eight section inspectors working under district officers based at Burslem, Market Drayton and Northwich, instead of six section inspectors working under technical officers based at Northwich.

The problems of the Trent & Mersey included that of subsidence, which had been 'increasing' as early as July 1882.[15] The mid-Cheshire area around Northwich had long been important for salt mining. A seam of natural rock salt had been discovered in the mid-seventeenth century on the Marbury estate near Northwich; and when the mine at Marston was worked out, water flooded it and the roof pillars collapsed. In 1779 the beds of rock salt at Thurlwood were developed, probably because of the proximity of the Trent & Mersey Canal. Lower and richer seams were discovered at Rode Heath and eventually, when these mines were flooded, brine pumping was used instead of mining. This continued in the Thurlwood area until 1927, when the works were abandoned because of severe subsidence which had caused the shaft to collapse. The River Wheelock, which ran alongside the works, changed its course and discharged some of its water down the shaft; attempts to divert the water were unsuccessful.

In the area around Marston the abandoned salt mines were

located about 50yd from the Trent & Mersey. In the mid-1930s subsidence began to affect the canal, and by 1939 it had affected the towpath very seriously. A few feet away from the towpath were four shafts which reached to a depth of 300ft. One of these had not been properly sealed, and this resulted in the enlargement of an underground cavern by salt solution, which caused the original brick lining of the shaft to collapse. The edge of the crater where the shaft reached the surface was dangerously near the canal wall, and attempts were made to block the shaft by dropping tons of material into the cavity. There was a constant danger that if the crater reached the canal an inflow of water would make a large hole and drain the canal's adjoining section.

At Thurlwood subsidence reached the upper locks in 1950, breaking the top gate and forebay. The towpath lock was badly cracked and had to be demolished. It was reconstructed in the traditional brick and masonry materials, and soon afterwards the offside lock was found to be damaged. This was reconstructed, but the towpath lock was again affected by subsidence, and by 1953 the damage was so extensive that it had to be demolished. The double arch bridge spanning the two locks at Thurlwood was also demolished, since it was found to be unsafe. A new bridge was designed, with pre-stressed concrete beams on concrete abutments; and it was decided that a steel lock should be constructed on specially prepared supports, which could be raised by jacking as further subsidence took place. The lock was 106ft long, 18ft wide and 45ft deep; and the steel tank was 72ft long, 7ft 9in wide and 18ft deep. The cost of the work was £61,000, and the contractors were Sir William Arrol & Co of Glasgow.

At Marston it was decided that a new length of canal should be cut to bypass the old salt-mine shaft. Work was begun in 1957 and completed in March 1958, and the new canal was 650yd long. As it was still in an area liable to subsidence, concrete walls 2ft thick and clay puddle cores 3ft thick were built behind the walls on the towpath and the offside throughout its length. The new line crossed the site of an old dry dock and a disused wet dock but these were severed completely from the new channels. Steel piling was used to cut off the old line from the new, and the old length of canal was filled in. The cost of the new cut, including the purchase of land, was £30,000; the contractors were George

Dew & Co of Oldham. The new cut at Marston and the steel lock at Thurlwood were opened by Lord Rusholme on 19 May 1958.[16] The complicated and expensive steel lock was not, however, a success, and it is now bypassed by means of the duplicate conventional chamber.

In 1958 the roof of Harecastle tunnel was raised, and part of the towpath was removed. Subsidence had created problems for many years because Harecastle hill was full of tunnels, not only railway and canal tunnels, but also mine-workings and culverts. Inside the tunnel there was extensive pollution from the old coal mines, and when the towpath was being removed, Ken Wedgwood, a foreman employed on the Potteries section, told *Waterways News* that conditions in the tunnel were 'foggy'. The men taking out the towpath came in from the south end, and the 'cutting-down gang' and the bricklayers came in from the north end. They had one bucket of water for their tea, and another to wash their hands in. They had no phones, and no contact with the outside world. Tilley lamps provided light, and the men worked on a platform made from railway sleepers. Their tools consisted of sledge hammers, cutting bars, picks and shovels. While the towpath was being removed and the roof was being repaired, traffic continued to use the Harecastle tunnel; the work was carried out on Saturday nights and on Sundays.

Pollution inside the tunnel continued, and in October 1957 because of a collapse in the old workings, the canal had to be closed while the tunnel was cleared of silt, tar and fumes.[17] After meetings with the Birchenwood Gas & Coke Co, it was decided in 1958 that the matter of pollution should be brought to the courts for an injunction against the nuisance. After consultation with the commercial pleasure-craft interest, reduced hours of working were introduced at Harecastle tunnel in May 1959. Meetings were held with the National Coal Board and the Birchenwood Co about the elimination of the ammonia liquid responsible for some of the pollution.[18]

The Bowes Committee of Inquiry into Inland Waterways reported in July 1958. It said that the principal traffic on the Trent & Mersey Canal was between the Mersey and the Potteries; the canal south of the Potteries was little used by commercial traffic. The canal was put into Class B, which meant that commercial craft carrying up to 60 tons should pay no tolls, but should be licensed annually on the basis of £1 per ton of capacity per annum. Canals in Class B were considered worth maintaining for transport purposes for at least twenty-five years, and the Committee recommended that Class B waterways should be restored to their greatest possible widths and depths, and that the worst obstacles should be removed. The financial position of the Trent & Mersey Canal was not encouraging:

| Year | Gross receipts (£) | Working expenses (£) | Deficit (£) |
|------|-----|-----|-----|
| 1955 | 48,678 | 114,115 | 65,437 |
| 1956 | 49,677 | 104,214 | 54,537 |

Despite the committee's recommendations, the government said that it was unable to give a twenty-five-year guarantee of maintenance; and it left the development of canals to local authorities and voluntary organisations.[19] In April 1959 the government appointed an Inland Waterways Redevelopment Committee to consider and make recommendations for the re-development of those waterways which were no longer commercially viable.

In 1958 British Transport Waterways acquired the Mersey Weaver & Ship Canal Carrying Co of Burslem, whose fleet of sixteen powered boats and eleven butty boats had carried traffic between Merseyside and the Potteries. The Mersey Weaver Co had been created as a subsidiary of the Salt Union, an amalgamation of Cheshire, Worcestershire and Teesside salt manufacturers formed in 1888. In 1935 the Salt Union had merged with ICI, but the Mersey Weaver boats had been handed over to the Shirley family who had run the company until 1958.

Pleasure craft were now becoming more numerous. In 1958 British Waterways constructed *Water Lapwing* as a day-boat with seating for forty-five to be used for regular trips during the Potteries' Wakes fortnight in August; and at Fradley a small building was let to Swan Line Cruisers. The Stanley Reservoir was made available to the British Transport Commission Yacht Club for dinghy sailing; and the amusement arcades and sporting rights on Rudyard Lake were let to Mrs Maynard, the widow of the proprietor.

In 1958 expenditure at £39,894 exceeded income by £5,936, largely because of loss of traffic in china clay and other pottery materials. Rail rates were reduced in 1957, and imports by canal from Weston Point Docks fell from 36,204 tons in 1957 to 31,179 tons in 1958. The gravel traffic between Burslem and Manchester came to an end because of the closing of the canal-side works at Manchester.[20]

Subsidence from coal-mining was becoming more serious in the Sideway and Longport areas, and this began to affect the Burslem arm. Transhipment of salt at Anderton ceased entirely in 1960, when Cerebos Ltd transferred their trade to road transport. A new base for pleasure-craft was established at Middlewich in that year, and at Stoke-on-Trent *Water Lapwing* was put into service as a day-boat for trips to Trentham. In 1961 a bill was prepared under which the Burslem arm of the Trent & Mersey could be closed to navigation. The main traffic on the canal was now in raw materials for the Potteries, coal being carried as a return loading. Local traffic between Cockshute siding and the Caldon Canal ceased in the autumn of 1960, when road access was provided for the mill there. In 1961 the Caldon Canal was dredged in an unsuccessful attempt to restart commercial coal-carrying to Froghall. A closure notice for the Caldon Canal appeared at Etruria, but was never implemented.[21]

The British Transport Act of 1962 abolished the British Transport Commission, and in its place a number of independent boards were set up. The British Waterways Board, a new statutory body responsible for the canals and navigable rivers administered by the commission, was now directly answerable to the Minister of Transport. The act empowered the board to close the Burslem arm to navigation, and this section of the canal was subsequently filled in. The board operated hire cruisers from Middlewich, but it became increasingly clear that the commercial traffic on the Trent & Mersey was being destroyed by the combined competition of road and rail. The tonnages carried to the Potteries by the Southern Fleet between 1959 and 1963 were as follows:[22]

| Year | Tonnage |
|------|---------|
| 1959 | 23,940 |
| 1960 | 23,006 |
| 1961 | 21,069 |
| 1962 | 13,839 |
| 1963 | 12,399 |

Slack was carried by canal to Henry Seddon's salt factory at

Middlewich until its closure in the 1960s. The last working boat was the *Tench*, which stopped operating in 1967.

In 1965 the British Waterways Board issued a volume entitled *The Facts about the Waterways*. This stated that the narrow-boat traffic between the Potteries and the Mersey was 'only small', the Shropshire Union being the preferred route. Because of its many connections, the Trent & Mersey was used as a cruising route; the most popular section was between the summit and Middlewich. The canal was relatively costly to maintain, because of brine subsidence in mid-Cheshire and extensive mining subsidence in the Rugeley and Stoke areas; subsidence was expected to get worse in Rugeley. The gross receipts in 1964 from Preston Brook to Dallow Lane lock at Burton were £50,888. This included £35,893 from water sales, most of which were from the northern length above Trentham lock. The revenue from commercial traffic on this length was £1,563, that from pleasure craft £4,147; the deficit was £42,442. Between Dallow Lane lock and Derwent Mouth the canal was used by pleasure craft, but there was no regular commercial traffic. The gross receipts in 1964 were £4,467, which included £3,240 from water sales in Burton; the deficit was £8,153. It was argued that the overall deficit could be reduced to about £30,000 if the whole canal was converted into a water channel;[23] but under the Transport Act of 1968 the Trent & Mersey was designated a cruiseway, which meant that navigation rights were safeguarded.

# 7

# The Survival of the
# Trent & Mersey Canal

During the 1960s and 1970s positive action was taken for the preservation of the canals; although it seemed unlikely that the Trent & Mersey would ever again be commercially viable on any large scale, it was recognised that it should be kept open to navigation and maintained in good order as a much-needed amenity.

The Caldon Canal seemed doomed in 1961, but in July of that year the canal was visited by the Inland Waterways Redevelopment Committee, the body set up to advise the Minister of Transport on disused canals. The scene of dereliction on the Caldon Canal presented a challenge to the committee members who tried to walk along the overgrown towpath; but they recognised that the canal was fulfilling a vital function in supplying water from its three reservoirs, and felt that it would be better if the canal could be restored for navigation. A band of devotees met in 1963, and formed a committee to work for the restoration of the Caldon Canal. They brought together such interested bodies as Staffordshire County Council and Stoke-on-Trent City Council, and the Caldon Canal Committee then became the Caldon Canal Society.

In 1967 a specially designed steel twin-hulled craft, the *Milton Maid*, was put into use on the Caldon Canal to carry ware from Johnson Brothers' four factories in Hanley to the packing house in Milton, four miles away. In August 1973 *Milton Queen*, a slightly larger narrow boat with a deck almost level with the water, was launched in order that greater use might be made of the canal. The new boat carried 20 tons, and cost £2,500; this was more than £1,000 less than the cost of a specially designed lorry trailer, which could carry only one-third of the cargo. Transport costs over the short distance were said to be less than half those of road transport, and breakages on pottery ware were reduced by over two-thirds.

In 1968 the Caldon Canal was classified as a 'remainder water-way' under the 1968 Transport Act. An agreement on the restoration of the canal was reached in 1972 between the British Waterways Board and the local authorities; but the branch from Norton to the ironworks and collieries was not included in this agreement. Many volunteers, including the members of the Caldon Canal Society and the Stoke-on-Trent Boat Club, worked for the restoration of the Caldon Canal; and on 28 September 1974 it was reopened for navigation as far as Froghall. The opening ceremony was performed at Cheddleton top lock. This lock and the Waterworks lock had been completely reconstructed, and major repairs had been carried out to many of the fourteen others. The piped section near Froghall, constructed in the early 1960s when there were serious landslips, had been replaced by a concrete channel.

At the reopening ceremony tributes were paid to the Caldon Canal Society, to the Stoke-on-Trent Corporation and the Staffordshire County Council, and to the employees of the board who had completed the restoration in record time. The official party travelled in a fleet of boats from Cheddleton to Consall Forge, where some of the old lime kilns remain. The restoration of the Leek branch was declared to be the next aim of the Caldon Canal Society. This canal ends on a stone aqueduct over the River Churnet, the last half mile having been purchased by the Leek Urban District Council and filled in and developed as an industrial estate. The feed-water from Rudyard Lake flows into the canal at the end of the aqueduct.[1]

In 1971 the roof of Armitage tunnel was removed, because it was affected by subsidence caused by coal being mined nearby. In place of the tunnel a bridge was built to carry the A513 across the canal.[2] In July 1973 remedial work in Harecastle tunnel was undertaken by Rock Services (Midlands) Ltd. Stainless steel rock bolts were used to stabilise areas affected by falls, and metal mesh was held in place by stainless steel straps and sprayed with concrete to stabilise the brickwork at the end of the repair job. Despite these efforts it became necessary to close the tunnel in

September 1973, because two falls of roof lining blocked the navigation. A new lining was formed in reinforced concrete, but after a survey by British Waterways' engineers it was found that a further seven areas of tunnel lining, affecting a total length of 141yd, were liable to collapse.

The contract for the second phase of the repair was awarded to Mowlem Northern Ltd. Their work consisted in removing decayed brickwork and reshaping the tunnel to restore headroom. The old bricks were replaced, and a 12in drainage layer of large rounded aggregate was packed behind the new brickwork, with PVC sheets between the aggregate and the lining to deflect water. One of the many problems was that the water which drained into the canal contained ochre which was highly corrosive. There were delays because worked-out coal seams had left a void above the old lining, and this had to be packed with Thermalite blocks. The second phase was completed in the autumn of 1975.

Working conditions inside the tunnel were very poor. There was a minimum of plant, and only five people could be accommodated in a very cramped situation. Fresh air was provided by a fan-chamber at the south entrance. Mowlem provided a floating work platform, strong enough to hold the five men and their equipment. British Waterways' engineers designed and constructed two work-boats to carry materials and equipment into the tunnel. The materials needed included not only bricks but also cement and grout for filling the voids; the boats also had to remove excavated material.

The third and final section of the work was let to Lehane Mackenzie & Shand, and the work was carried out by Shand (Midlands). There were four sections to repair, and the work began in January 1976. Chris Benbow, the manager of Shand (Midlands), told the editor of *Waterways News* that their main concern was for the safety of their men, and that they opened up only 3ft at a time and built an 18in length of lining each day. The strata behind the lining were very unstable and were liable to collapse. The men worked on platforms called unifloats, but in places the tunnel was too narrow to accommodate these 8ft wide platforms, which then had to be towed into place on their sides and placed the right way up. Each platform was made up of two floats joined together, and two or three men worked on each platform with a generator, a compressor, a small concrete mixer and materials.

The men had a canteen and a GPO telephone inside the tunnel. One of the dangers was that the removal of the tunnel lining might reveal one of Telford's fifteen construction shafts and cause a flow of materials within the shaft; the board's engineers therefore undertook to locate these shafts, of which no trace existed either on the surface or in the tunnel. The work was slowly and arduously completed over a period of three and a half years; and on 2 April 1977 the Harecastle tunnel was reopened by Sir Frank Price, the Chairman of the British Waterways Board, whose party navigated the tunnel from north to south in the passenger-boat *Lapwing*. The long closure had caused anxiety in some quarters, but the restoration of the tunnel, at a cost of well over £100,000, restored faith in the British Waterways Board's determination to maintain and extend cruising waterways. Further brickwork repairs had still to be carried out in the tunnel; these consisted mainly in replacing perished brickwork at water-level, and were to be carried out by employees of the British Waterways Board.[3]

During these extensive repairs no one complained of having encountered the 'Kidsgrove Boggart', the headless ghost of a woman who had been murdered in the middle of the tunnel. According to one account she had been killed by a boatman who hid her body in a coal-loading stage called Gilbert's Hole; the body was later discovered, and the boatman was tried and executed. The ghost's piercing screams and appearance in neighbouring woods were long regarded as foretelling disaster in the nearby collieries. Another version attributed the murder to two men, and said that the body had been thrown into the water; according to this account, the ghost could appear either as a white horse or as a headless female. No contemporary reports of the crime have come to light, and the traditional stories offer different estimates of its date. Some versions assign it to the early nineteenth century, in which case Brindley's tunnel would be the scene of the crime; but others place it between 1827 and the railway's arrival in the late 1840s.

Passenger traffic was never important on the Trent & Mersey, but the legend may have originated in the tragic story of Christina Collins, a young woman in her early thirties who, in June 1839, was travelling by canal from Liverpool to join her husband in London. She boarded one of Pickford's fly-boats at Preston

Brook and, as the journey proceeded, the crew of three men became very drunk. After raping and murdering Mrs Collins, they threw her body into the water; two of them were executed, and the third was transported for life. There was also a boy in the boat, but he was not incriminated. The case was reported on 22 and 29 June 1839 in the *Staffordshire Advertiser*, where it was argued that it showed the need for greater stringency and discipline among canal employees.[4]

Etruria, at the junction with the Caldon Canal, has been regarded as the possible centre for a museum and amenity area. The Etruscan Bone and Flint Mill built in 1857 has been envisaged as a museum of industrial archaeology, with the working beam engine as its highlight; and there have been proposals for an inland waterways museum in the old canal workshops. The graving dock and maintenance yard would remain in service, and there would be mooring sites and service facilities for pleasure craft. All that remains of the Etruria Wedgwood Pottery works is one small, forlorn circular building. The works were sold in 1943 to Shelton Iron, Steel & Coal Co, who subsequently took a lease of the premises; and in 1951 the lease was sold to the Dunlop Rubber Co. Subsidence caused the long range of three-storey buildings fronting the canal to be 12ft below water. At one time a row of cottages for employees continued along the canal from the works, but these were replaced after 1844 by an extension to the works. By 1892 the Shelton Iron, Steel & Coal Co were using Etruria Hall as offices, and in 1930 they bought the Hall from the Duchy of Lancaster. The Hall is still occupied by this company which, since 1956, has been known as Shelton Iron & Steel Ltd. In 1939 the Wedgwood factory moved to a site close to the canal at Barlaston; the facilities there now include a visitors' centre, a museum, a cinema and a shop.[5] The bottle kilns which were once a distinctive feature of the Potteries are no longer in use; but a few are still preserved as relics of the past.

The link with the Derby Canal at Swarkestone was severed in 1964, when the Derby Canal was abandoned and drained; but the attractive toll-house at the junction has been preserved as the headquarters of the Swarkestone Boat Club.

In 1974, as part of its aim of restoring and preserving the canal, the newly formed Trent & Mersey Canal Society joined in a campaign to make Shardlow a conservation area; in May 1975 the canal port was designated a conservation area by Derbyshire County Council and South Derbyshire District Council. The overgrown basin of no 2 mill was cleaned and dredged, and the mill was restored; it is now occupied by a hire-boat firm.[6]

The Anderton lift celebrated its centenary in 1975; in the previous year it had been given a major overhaul, which involved the replacement of corroded girders. In 1975 the Civic Trust gave the British Waterways Board an award for excellence in the field of urban and architectural conservation; this was based partly on the repairs to the Anderton lift and partly on improvements to the Middlewich wharf and to the Red Bull Yard in Northwich.[7]

Efforts to preserve the old salt warehouse at Horninglow Road in Burton-on-Trent were unsuccessful, despite the fact that the warehouse was probably the earliest canal warehouse to survive in Burton. It had been altered in the late nineteenth century, and was not included in the statutory list of buildings of special architectural or historic interest; the Horninglow road improvement scheme required its demolition, and large sums would have been needed to preserve it.[8]

Because of the construction of an urban motorway known as the Stoke 'D' Road, the single bridge crossing the Trent & Mersey at Liverpool Road interchange had to be replaced by three road-bridges and a foot-bridge; and in order to make room for these, 220yd of the canal had to be diverted and a new lock and lock-house had to be constructed. The canal diversion was begun in July 1976, and after a public meeting held in Stoke Town Hall an eight-week closure of the canal was agreed to. The work was completed in the sixth week of the stoppage, and on 28 August 1976 the canal was reopened.[9]

In May 1977 the bicentenary of the Trent & Mersey Canal was celebrated in a rally organised by the Trent & Mersey Canal Society at Barlaston, on land beside the canal owned by the Wedgwood Co. The celebrations included music, dancing, displays, a tug-of-war, and the roasting of a whole ox; and the Lord Lieutenant of Staffordshire fired a siege cannon across the canal, in memory of the firing of a cannon in 1771 to mark the opening of the canal to Stone.[10] Josiah Wedgwood and James Brindley would have been pleased to know that their canal was still being honoured in this way after a working life of two hundred years.

# Acknowledgements

One of the difficulties in writing a history of the Trent & Mersey Canal was that the material was fragmentary and scattered. I am, therefore, especially grateful to the British Academy, who gave me a grant towards the expenses of research. The task was made more pleasant by the ready co-operation and help I received from many libraries and record offices, several of whose officers undertook work beyond what could reasonably have been expected. I should like to thank in particular the public libraries of Birmingham, Derby, Manchester, Shrewsbury, Stoke-on-Trent and Stratford-on-Avon, the university libraries in Bangor, Cambridge, Keele, Leicester, Manchester and Nottingham, and the record offices of Cheshire, Derbyshire, Shropshire and Staffordshire. I was also given much help by the Institution of Civil Engineers, and by Mr Richard Hutchings, the Curator of the Waterways Museum at Stoke Bruerne. Messrs Josiah Wedgwood & Sons Ltd and Royal Doulton Tableware Ltd responded willingly to requests for help, as did the Caldon Canal Society and the Trent & Mersey Canal Society. I am grateful also for the help given by Professor T. C. Barker, Dr W. H. Chaloner, Mrs Margaret Clark, Mr Chris Davies, Ms Sheila Doig, Mr M. Handford, Mr A. W. Jeffery, Professor A. H. John, Dr R. S. Fitton, Mr Peter Lead, Dr Hugh Malet, Mrs F. W. Pratt, Dr H. C. Torrens and Mr Philip Weaver.

Mr Charles Hadfield suggested that I write the book, and lent me his valuable collection of notes. I am indebted to him for many helpful suggestions and tactful corrections; but any remaining errors are of course my own responsibility. Until her death in 1976, my mother took a keen interest in the work. I should like to thank my brother John and his wife Mollie for their encouragement. My husband and children have, as always, been unfailingly helpful.

# Notes

Abbreviations used: BTHR—British Transport Historical Records; CRO—County Records Office; *DNB—Dictionary of National Biography; JHC—Journals of the House of Commons;* NSR—North Staffordshire Railway; *VCHS—Victoria County History of Stafford*

## Notes to Chapter 1

1. See *Gentleman's Magazine* 36, March 1766, p. 141.
2. Wedgwood Collection, Keele University Library (by permission of Messrs Josiah Wedgwood & Sons Ltd, Barlaston).
3. M. W. Greenslade and J. G. Jenkins, *VCHS* 2, 1967, pp. 80 and 253.
4. John Thomas, *The Rise of the Staffordshire Potteries,* 1971, p. 3.
5. W. J. Thompson, *Industrial Archaeology of North Staffordshire,* 1976, p. 90.
6. T. K. Derry and Trevor I. Williams, *A Short History of Technology,* 1960, p. 585, and *VCHS* 2, p. 12.
7. Paul Mantoux, *The Industrial Revolution in the Eighteenth Century,* 1961, p. 124.
8. M. Drabble, *Arnold Bennett,* 1974, p. 23; C. T. G. Boucher, *James Brindley, Engineer, 1716–1772,* 1968, p. 23.
9. S. Smiles, *Lives of the Engineers,* 1, 1874, pp. 171 and 227; Boucher, op. cit., p. 86; see also W. H. Chaloner, 'James Brindley and his Remuneration', *Transactions of the Lancashire and Cheshire Antiquarian Society* 75 and 76, 1965–6.
10. Smiles, op. cit., 1, pp. 148 and 154.
11. *Derby Mercury,* 7 December 1758; CRO Stafford D 593/H/9/1; Norton 1005 (1804), Central Libraries Birmingham.
12. *Collected Reports of John Smeaton* 1, pp. 13–17, 11 July 1761.
13. Hugh Malet, *The Canal Duke,* 1961, pp. 29, 55, 58 and 108; Hugh Malet 'The Duke of Bridgewater and the eighteenth-century fuel crisis', *Local History Research,* 1974, p. 8.
14. John Aiken, *A Description of the Country from Thirty to Forty Miles Round Manchester,* 1975 reprint, p. 117.
15. Information about John Hardman supplied by S. A. Harris.
16. *A Short View of the General Advantages of Inland Navigation with a Plan of a Navigable Canal Intended for the Communication between the Ports of Liverpool and Hull,* Wedgwood Collection 24151–32, pp.9 and 13.
17. Wedgwood Collection, Keele University Library.
18. Sir James A. Picton, *City of Liverpool Municipal Archives and Records from 1700 to 1835,* 1886, p. 243.
19. *Derby Mercury,* 7 December 1758.
20. Charles Hadfield, *The Canals of the West Midlands,* 1966, p. 19.
21. Wedgwood Collection, Keele University Library.
22. J. Wedgwood to T. Bentley, 26 September 1765, Wedgwood Collection, Keele University Library.
23. Mantoux, op. cit., pp. 128 and 382–3.
24. *DNB*; Mantoux, op. cit., p. 384; J. Ward, *Borough of Stoke-on-Trent,* 1843, p. 434.
25. T. S. Willan, *The Navigation of the River Weaver in the Eighteenth Century,* 1951, p. 90.

26. J. Wedgwood to T. Bentley, 2 January 1765, Wedgwood Collection, Keele University Library.
27. J. Wedgwood to T. Bentley, 23 December 1765, transcript of Wedgwood Correspondence 1101–1108, John Rylands Library, Manchester.
28. S. Garbett to J. Wedgwood, Wedgwood Collection, Keele University Library.
29. Hadfield, op. cit., pp. 40–41.
30. E. Dane, *The Economic History of the Staffordshire Pottery Inudstry to 1850*, unpublished MA thesis, University of Sheffield, 1929.
31. Hadfield, op. cit., p. 19.
32. Willan, op. cit., p. 136.
33. Wedgwood Collection, Keele University Library. I am indebted to Mr. C. Davies who allowed me to read his unpublished article, 'The Grand Trunk Canal Project. Eighteenth century transport politics and promotion.'
34. Wedgwood Collection, Keele University Library.
35. Wedgwood Collection, Keele University Library.
36. Wedgwood Collection, Keele University Library.
37. Hadfield, op. cit., p. 22.
38. J. Phillips, *General History of Inland Navigation*, 1970 reprint, pp. 117–21.
39. Willan, op. cit., pp. 91–92 and 198.
40. 6 July 1765, Wedgwood Collection, Keele University Library.
41. 12 December 1765, Wedgwood Collection, Keele University Library; Hugh Malet, *Bridgewater, the Canal Duke, 1736–1803*, 1977, p. 110.
42. Willan, op. cit., pp. 199–204.
43. Wedgwood Correspondence, John Rylands Library, Manchester.
44. *JHC* XXX, 15 January and 7 February 1766, pp. 451 and 519–20.
45. *JHC* XXX, 15 January 1766, p. 453.
46. *JHC* XXX, 10 and 26 February and 3 March 1766, pp. 522–3, 605 and 618.
47. *JHC* XXX, 18, 24 and 27 March 1766, pp. 668–9, 686 and 701; see also W. H. Chaloner, 'Charles Roe of Macclesfield (1715–81): An eighteenth century Industrialist', *Transactions of the Lancashire and Cheshire Antiquarian Society* 62, 1950–51, p. 148.
48. *Journals of the House of Lords* XXXI, pp. 350 and 353; Chaloner, op. cit., pp. 155–6.
49. *Aris's Birmingham Gazette*, 28 April 1766.
50. Chaloner, op. cit., p. 156.
51. *JHC* XXX, 8 February, 10 and 14 April 1766, pp. 707, 713–14, 720–21.
52. *JHC* XXX, 12 March 1766, p. 649.
53. 6 Geo III c 96, 14 May 1766, sections 59 and 60; Willan, op. cit., p. 97.
54. Ibid., p. 93.
55. Smiles, op. cit., 1, pp. 264–5.
56. *VCHS* 8, p. 144; Henry Wedgwood, *The Romance of Staffordshire*, 1879, p. 82.

## Notes to Chapter 2

1. Wedgwood Correspondence, John Rylands Library, Manchester; Alexander Chisholm's copy of Josiah Wedgwood's notes on canals in his *Commonplace Book*, p. 264 (History Faculty Library, Cambridge). I am indebted to Mr. C. Davies for this latter reference.
2. Wedgwood Correspondence, John Rylands Library, Manchester.
3. Charles Hadfield, *The Canals of the West Midlands*, 1966, pp. 42–4.
4. Wedgwood Correspondence, John Rylands Library, Manchester; information supplied by Mrs. Margaret Clark.
5. W. J. Thompson, *Industrial Archaeology of North Staffordshire*, 1976, p. 21.
6. L. T. C. Rolt, *Navigable Waterways*, 1973, pp. 42–3.
7. Sir Joseph Banks, *Journal of a Journey through Wales and the Midlands in 1767–8* (Cambridge University Library Add MS 6294 NP), p. 85; Telford MSS 15 (Institution of Civil Engineers).
8. *Aris's Birmingham Gazette*, 14 September 1767.
9. *Derby Mercury*, 6 October 1768.

10. *Nicholson's Guides to the Waterways*, 4, *North-East*, n.d., p. 40.
11. Arthur Young, *Tour through the North of England* 3, 1771, p. 257.
12. S. Smiles, *Lives of the Engineers* 1, 1874, p. 269; *General History of Inland Navigation*, 1803, iv, quoted in W. H. Chaloner, 'John Phillips: surveyor and writer on canals', *Transport History* 5, no. 2, July 1972, p. 168.
13. Charles Hadfield, *The Canals of the East Midlands*, 1966, pp. 15–16.
14. Wedgwood Correspondence, John Rylands Library, Manchester.
15. *JHC* XXXII, pp. 723–4, 836 and 843.
16. Hugh Malet, *The Canal Duke*, 1961, pp. 120–27.
17. *Derby Mercury*, 20 April 1770.
18. *Derby Mercury*, 7 September, 1770.
19. *Aris's Birmingham Gazette*, 18 and 25 November 1771.
20. Sir James A. Picton, *City of Liverpool Municipal Archives and Records from 1700 to 1835*, 1886, p. 244.
21. Wedgwood Correspondence, John Rylands Library, Manchester.
22. E. J. D. Warrillow, *History of Etruria*, 1952, pp. 133–40.
23. Wedgwood Correspondence, John Rylands Library, Manchester.
24. Warrillow, op. cit., p. 26.
25. Smiles, op. cit., 1, pp. 286–8.
26. *Gentleman's Magazine* 36, January 1766, p. 33 and 42, October 1772, p. 495.
27. Wedgwood Correspondence, John Rylands Library, Manchester.
28. CRO Stafford HM 37/19.
29. *Derby Mercury*, 16 April 1773.
30. Smiles, op. cit., 1, p. 266.
31. *Derby Mercury*, 26 November 1773.
32. CRO Stafford HM 37/19.
33. Wedgwood Correspondence, John Rylands Library, Manchester.
34. W. R. Dawson, *The Banks Letters* (British Museum, Natural History), 1958; *Derby Mercury*, 14 November 1793. I am indebted to Mr. D. H. Tew for the former reference.
35. Wedgwood Correspondence, John Rylands Library, Manchester; Hadfield, *The Canals of the West Midlands*, p. 33.
36. Wedgwood Correspondence, John Rylands Library, Manchester.
37. Shaw's 'Tour to the West of England', pp. 317–18 in *A General Collection of the Best and Most Interesting Voyages and Travels* 2, 1808.
38. *JHC* XXXV, 7 March 1775, p. 176, 13 April 1775 p. 229; CRO Stafford D 554/162.
39. CRO Stafford HM 37/40; Alexander Chisholm's copy of Wedgwood's notes on canals in his *Commonplace Book*, pp. 331–3.
40. T. S. Willan, *The Navigation of the River Weaver in The Eighteenth Century*, 1951, p. 109.
41. *Aris's Birmingham Gazette*, 21 July 1777.
42. C. T. G. Boucher, *James Brindley, Engineer, 1716–1772*, 1968, p. 80; Hadfield, *The Canals of the West Midlands*, p. 32.
43. Wedgwood Correspondence, John Rylands Library, Manchester; Wedgwood Collection, Keele University Library; J. R. Ward, *The Finance of Canal Building in Eighteenth Century England*, 1974, pp. 28 and 128.
44. Smiles, op. cit., 1, pp. 251 and 273–4.
45. T. Pennant, *The Journey from Chester to London*, 1782, pp. 55–6.
46. *Derby Mercury*, 20 March 1783.

## Notes to Chapter 3

1. Wedgwood Correspondence, John Rylands Library, Manchester.
2. J. Farey, *A General View of the Agriculture of Derbyshire* 3, 1817, pp. 435–6.
3. CRO Stafford, D 554/162.
4. *JHC* XXXV, 12 February 1776, p. 548.
5. *JHC* XXXV, 19 March 1776, pp. 663–4.
6. *JHC* XXXV, 18 April 1776, p. 706.

7. *JHC* XXXV, 24 April 1776, pp. 717–18.
8. CRO Stafford, Meeting of the Committee of the Trent & Mersey Canal, 13 June 1776, D 554/162.
9. A. Burton and D. Pratt, *Canals in Colour*, 1974, p. 174; *Nicholson's Guides to the Waterways*, 2, *North-west*, n.d., pp. 93–8; Charles Hadfield, *The Canals of the West Midlands*, 1966, p. 34.
10. Farey, op. cit., 3, pp. 445–6; Rees's *Cyclopaedia* 4, 1819; Peter Lead, 'The Caldon Canal 1778–1978', *Cherry Eye*, Caldon Canal Society, no. 3, 1976–7.
11. Farey, op. cit., 3, p. 436.
12. Hadfield, op. cit., p. 34.
13. CRO Stafford, HM 37/19; Alexander Chisholm's copy of Wedgwood's *Commonplace Book* (History Faculty Library, Cambridge).
14. Farey, op. cit., 3, pp. 436–9; Hadfield, op. cit., p. 201.
15. Dr. and Mrs. A. E. Dodd, 'The Froghall-Uttoxeter Canal', *North Staffordshire Journal of Field Studies* 3, 1963; C. M. Beardmore, 'The Uttoxeter Canal', *Cherry Eye*, nos. 1, 1975, and 3, 1976–7; W. Parsons, and T. Bradshaw, *Staffs General Directory for 1818*, pt. 2; Hadfield, op. cit., pp. 200–201; *Derby Mercury*, 16 September 1813, 25 August, 8 September 1824 and 19 June 1839.
16. *JHC* LII, 7 December 1796, p. 164.
17. Hadfield, op. cit., p. 200.
18. *Aris's Birmingham Gazette*, 18 November 1793; *The Caldon Canal*, booklet published by the Caldon Canal Society, n.d.
19. George Unwin, *Samuel Oldknow and the Arkwrights*, 1924, pp. 223–9.
20. Hadfield, op. cit., pp. 210–12; Frank Nixon, *Industrial Archaeology of Derbyshire*, 1969, p. 156; *Nicholson's Guides to the Waterways* 2, pp. 99–100; Telford MSS (Institution of Civil Engineers), T/TR 68, 109 and 116; 1 Will IV c 55; BTHR, Trent & Mersey minutes 14 April 1857.
21. Hadfield, op. cit., p. 181; *Nicholson's Guides to the Waterways* 2, p. 46; J. Priestley, *An Historical Account of the Navigable Rivers, Canals and Railways throughout Great Britain*, 1831, p. 685; BTHR Trent & Mersey minutes, 14 April 1857.
22. *Eddowes Salopian Journal*, 6 January 1798 and 2 January 1799; Hadfield, op. cit., p. 150.
23. *JHC* LII, 24 February 1797, p. 335 and LVII, 15 February 1802, p. 113; Hadfield, op. cit., pp. 201–2; S. Shaw, *History of the Staffordshire Potteries*, 1829, pp. 40 and 60.
24. William Molyneux, *Burton-on-Trent: Its History, Its Waters and Its Breweries*, 1869, pp. 114–15, 224 and 229; Report to the General Assembly, 1787 and 1790, CRO Stafford, 37/19; CRO Stafford, Q/RU M 15; Charles Hadfield, *The Canals of the East Midlands*, 1966, p. 77; *JHC* L, 6 February, 19 March, 9 and 22 April 1795, pp. 160, 340–1, 406 and 457.

## Notes to Chapter 4

1. Robert Sherlock, *Industrial Archaeology of Staffordshire*, 1976, p. 41; S. Shaw, *History of the Staffordshire Potteries*, 1829, pp. 4, 10–11; *Derby Mercury*, 6 November 1800.
2. J. R. Ward, *The Finance of Canal Building in Eighteenth Century England*, 1974, p. 120; Charles Hadfield, *The Canals of the East Midlands*, 1966, pp. 19–24; CRO Stafford, Reports, 1785, 1786, 1787, 1788 and 1789, HM 37/19.
3. CRO Stafford, Report 1790, HM 37/19.
4. Hadfield, op. cit., pp. 67–9; BTHR, HRP 6/15/19.
5. *JHC* XXXIV, 13 April 1775, p. 309, L, 5 February 1795, pp. 147, 224, 336, 341, 426 and 427; Charles Hadfield, *The Canals of the West Midlands*, 1966, pp. 40 and 206.
6. *VCHS* 8, pp. 1–3, Hadfield, *The Canals of the West Midlands*, pp. 206–9; Peter Lead, 'The proposed inclined plane at Newcastle-under-Lyme', *Journal of the Railway and Canal Historical Society* 20, no. 3, November 1974.
7. 'The Commercial Canal Project', 1796, Stoke-on-Trent City Library; Hadfield, *The Canals of the West Midlands*, p. 198; Hadfield, *The Canals of the East Midlands*, pp. 116–17.

8. Alexander Chisholm's copy of Wedgwood's notes in his *Commonplace Book* (History Faculty Library, Cambridge): abbreviated notes from the reports on canals mentioned in the minutes of the potters' committee, pp. 241–7 and 257; L. T. C. Rolt, *Navigable Waterways*, 1973, p. 155; CRO Stafford, Report 1786 HM 37/19.

9. T. S. Willan, *The Navigation of the River Weaver in the Eighteenth Century*, 1951, pp. 110–11, 116–18 and 129–33; Wedgwood's *Commonplace Book*, p. 157.

10. *Aris's Birmingham Gazette*, 1 May 1780; Josiah Wedgwood and some of the committee, *Some Considerations on the Expediency of the Proprietors of the Navigation from the Trent to the Mersey acting as Carriers upon the Canal*, n.d. but *c.* 1785; Josiah Wedgwood, *A State of Facts respecting some Differences which have arisen betwixt his Grace the Duke of Bridgewater and the Proprietors of the Navigation from the Trent to the Mersey*, 1785; 'A letter to the Proprietors of the Canal from the Trent to the Mersey', Wedgwood Collection, Keele University Library; Committee of Commerce Minutes, in Wedgwood's *Commonplace Book*; William Jessop's letter in the possession of Mr. J. Brynmor Jones.

11. *Gentleman's Magazine* 65, January and October 1795, pp. 84–5 and 821–2; Wedgwood Correspondence, John Rylands Library, Manchester; Winifred Gérin, *Elizabeth Gaskell*, 1976, pp. 25–6; *DNB*.

12. 15 Geo III c 20; 23 Geo III c 33; BTHR, 2/2C List of Shareholders and Mortgagees; Wedgwood Collection, Keele University Library, 32/24177.

13. 'Present State of Stock', 1783/4, CRO Stafford; Reports of the General Assembly, 29 March 1785, 26 September 1786, 25 September 1787, 30 September 1788, 29 September 1789 and 28 September 1790, CRO Stafford, HM 37/19.

14. *Gentleman's Magazine*, 1810–1831.

15. Ward, op. cit., p. 19; Birmingham Public Libraries, Homer 346.

16. CRO Stafford, HM 37/19.

17. Wedgwood Collection, Keele University Library.

18. CRO Stafford, HM 37/19; CRO Salop, 212/Box 366.

19. Robert J. Wilson, *Knobsticks*, 1974, pp. 1–5; Wedgwood Collection, Keele University Library, 32/24179 and 110/20900; Williams, *Commercial Directory for Stafford and the Potteries*, 1846; CRO Derbyshire, Waybill 31 October 1831; BTHR Minutes 1, Trent & Mersey Canal Committee, 5 October 1852; Minutes of the Committee of the Weaver Trustees, No 480, quoted in F. C. Mather, *After the Canal Duke*, 1970, p. 125; Weaver's Navigation Minute Book, August 1822–July 1837, LNW 2/10, CRO Cheshire; W. H. Chaloner, 'Salt in Cheshire', *Transactions of the Lancashire and Cheshire Antiquarian Society* 71, 1961, p. 73.

20. John Byng, *The Torrington Diaries*, 1954, p. 192; Roy Christian, 'An Inland Port of the Canal Age', *Country Life*, 9 November 1961; Information supplied by Frank Nixon; J. Lee, 'The Rise and Fall of a Market Town', *Leicestershire Archaeological Society Transactions* 32, pp. 55–6; C. C. Owen, 'The Early History of the Upper Trent Navigation', *Transport History* 1, no. 3; Ronald Russell, *Waterside Pubs*, 1974, p. 113; *Derby Mercury*, 15 May 1839.

21. *Staffordshire Directory*, 1802; *VCHS* 8, pp. 84, 99 and 106.

22. CRO Cheshire, DMD/A/21.

23. *Staffordshire Advertiser*, 14 April 1798.

24. CRO Cheshire QD P22.

25. Byng, op. cit., p. 440; Shaw, op. cit., p. 33; *Chester Chronicle*, 2 January 1818; Henry Wedgwood, *The Romance of Staffordshire*, 1879, pp. 75–6; *VCHS* 8, p. 152.

26. Eva Broadbridge, 'Stone Survey', *Journal of the Staffordshire Industrial Archaeological Society*, no. 4, Spring 1973.

27. CRO Stafford, M 743, Telford MSS (Institution of Civil Engineers) 15, T/TR 1.

28. T/TR 2.

29. CRO Salop, 212/box 366.

30. T/TR 12; J. Rickman, *The Life of Thomas Telford*, 1832, p. 75.

31. T/TR 18.

32. T/TR 21 and 22.

33. T/TR 30 and 44.

34. T/TR 49.

35. T/TR 61.
36. T/TR 65.
37. T/TR 69.
38. T/TR 109; Report quoted in *Waterways News*, no. 69, May 1977.
39. T/TR 113; S. Smiles, *Lives of the Engineers* 3, 1874, p. 240.
40. T/TR 49, 80, 88, 91, 95, 98, 106 and 117.
41. Hadfield, *The Canals of the East Midlands*, p. 123; CRO Stafford, M7 43.

## Notes to Chapter 5

1. Michael Robbins, *The Railway Age*, 1965, p. 29; Jack Simmons, *The Railways of Britain*, 1961, p. 5.
2. *Aris's Birmingham Gazette*, 11 April 1825; *VCHS* 8, p. 209.
3. CRO Stafford, HM 37/19.
4. *Derby Mercury*, 10 October 1832.
5. *Derby Mercury*, 16 April 1834 and 12 October 1836.
6. J. Ward, *The Borough of Stoke-on-Trent*, 1843, p. 389.
7. Loch-Egerton Papers, quoted in F. C. Mather, *After the Canal Duke*, 1970, pp. 127–8.
8. *Derby Mercury*, 2 May 1838, 10 April 1839, 22 May 1839, 29 April 1840, 14 October 1840, 15 December 1841, 17 July 1844 and 24 December 1845.
9. BTHR NSR Report, 23 September 1846.
10. Second Report of the Select Committee on Canal and Railway Amalgamation, with Minutes of Evidence, 6 May 1846, in *Transport and Communications* 7 (Irish University Press), pp. 51 and 57–9.
11. NSR Report, 23 September 1846.
12. NSR Report, 1 July 1847.
13. Worcester & Birmingham Canal Committee Minute Book, 11 February, 19 May 1848, quoted in Charles Hadfield, *The Canals of the West Midlands*, 1966, p. 223.
14. Third Report of the Select Committee on Canal and Railway Amalgamation, in *Transport and Communications* 9, pp. 25, 29, 30 and 31; Mather, op. cit., pp. 201–2.
15. Robert J. Wilson, *Knobsticks*, 1974, pp. 6–10.
16. Eva Broadbridge, 'Stone Survey', *Journal of the Staffordshire Industrial Arachaeological Society*, no. 4, Spring 1973, pp. 15–17; H. Hanson, *The Canal Boatmen*, 1975.
17. Mather, op. cit., pp. 138–9; BTHR Minutes 1 1852–1858.
18. BTHR 1.
19. Third Report of the Select Committee on Canal and Railway Amalgamation, in *Transport and Communications* 9, pp. 13, 16–17, 69, and 118.
20. BTHR 1.
21. NSR Reports 1846–1854; *Royal Commission on Railways*, Minutes of Evidence, I, 1867, in *Transport and Communications* 10, p. 669.
22. BTHR 1.
23. BTHR 1; Hadfield, op. cit., p. 224; Mather, op. cit., p. 277.
24. BTHR 1.
25. *VCHS* 1, p. 291 and 2, p. 35.
26. BTHR 1; Mather, op. cit., pp. 258–60, 281, 296, 298 and 300.
27. Hadfield, op. cit., pp. 209–10 and 217–18.
28. Ibid., pp. 218–19; *VCHS* 8, pp. 179–80.
29. Hadfield, op. cit., p. 220.
30. Mather, op. cit., p. 301.
31. NSR Report, February 1862; *Royal Commission on Railways* 10, pp. 666–70.

## Notes to Chapter 6

1. BTHR Minutes 2, Trent & Mersey Navigation.
2. *The London Gazette*, 21 November 1871; 25 and 26 Vict c 98; CRO Cheshire, QDP 502.
3. Hugh McKnight, *The Shell Book of Inland Waterways*, 1975, p. 49.

4. *Report of the Select Committee on Railway Companies Amalgamation* 13, 1872, p. 1025; *Minutes of Evidence of the Select Committee on Railway Companies Amalgamation* 12, 1872, pp. 411 and XXVI.
5. NSR Report 2, 6 February 1874.
6. NSR Report 2; J. R. Hollick, 'The Caldon Low Tramways', a paper read to the Cheadle Historical Society, 24 March 1954.
7. NSR Report 2; *Minutes of Evidence of the Royal Commission on the Canals and Inland Navigation of the U.K.*, 1 (pt II) 1906, pp. 83–4; *Nicholson's Guides to the Waterways* 2, *North-west*, n.d., p. 88.
8. NSR Report 2; *Minutes of Evidence of the Royal Commission on the Canals and Inland Navigation of the U.K.* 1 (pt II) pp. 83–93, 153–4; see also Peter K. Roberts, 'The Harecastle Electric Tugs', *Journal of the Railway and Canal Historical Society*, 24, no. 2, July 1978; Peter Norton, 'Life at Preston Brook', *Journal of the Railway and Canal Historical Society* 22, no. 3, November 1976, pp. 95–6; Charles Hadfield, *The Canals of the West Midlands*, 1966, p. 228; 'Potts Profile', *Waterways News*, no. 68, April 1977.
9. *Fourth Report of the Royal Commission on Canals*, 1910, pp. 146–7.
10. Hollick, op. cit.; Hadfield, op. cit., pp. 229–30.
11. Philip S. Bagwell, *The Transport Revolution from 1770*, 1974, pp. 238, 240–44 and 247.
12. H. Hanson, *The Canal Boatmen*, 1975, p. 97; L. T. C. Rolt, *Navigable Waterways*, 1973, pp. 161–2; Robert J. Wilson, *Knobsticks*, 1974, pp. 11 and 26.
13. Bagwell, op. cit., p. 303; Hadfield, op. cit., p. 230; *The Caldon Canal*, booklet issued by the Caldon Canal Society, n.d.
14. *The Report of the Board of Survey on Canals and Inland Waterways*, 1955, pp. 30, 31 and 69.
15. British Transport Waterways, Report, 1956, pp. 10 and 14–15; NSR 2 and 26, July 1882.
16. Pamphlet, 'Opening of Thurlwood Lock and Marston New Cut, Trent & Mersey Canal', British Waterways, 19 May 1958; British Transport Waterways, Reports, 1956, p. 10, 1957, p. 10 and 1958, p. 8.
17. *Waterways News*, no. 69, May 1977.
18. British Transport Waterways, Reports, 1958 and 1959.
19. *The Bowes Report of the Committee of Inquiry into Inland Waterways*, 1958, pp. 17, 29 and 104.
20. British Transport Waterways, Report, 1958, pp. 3, 4, 5, 9 and 14; Wilson, op. cit., p. 11.
21. British Transport Waterways, Reports, 1960, pp. 5 and 6–7, 1961, pp. 3, 4 and 11.
22. British Transport Waterways, Reports, 1959, p. 4, 1960, pp. 4, 5 and 6, 1961, pp. 4 and 11, 1962, p. 4, 1963, p. 4.
23. Anon., *The Facts about the Waterways*, 1965, pp. 108–109.

## Notes to Chapter 7

1. *The Caldon Canal*, booklet published by the Caldon Canal Society, n.d.; information supplied by Messrs Wedgwood Ltd; *Waterways News*, no. 49, August 1975.
2. *Nicholson's Guides to the Waterways* 2, *North-west*, p. 77.
3. *Waterways News*, no. 65, January 1977, and no. 69, May 1977.
4. *Towpath*, January–February 1975, pp. 6–8; H. Hanson, *The Canal Boatmen*, 1975, p. 71.
5. *VCHS* 8, pp. 150 and 166; *Waterways News*, no. 69, May 1977.
6. *Towpath*, January–February 1975, pp. 9–10; *Waterways News*, no. 72, September 1977.
7. *Waterways News*, no. 49, August 1975.
8. *Towpath*, March–April 1977.
9. *Waterways News*, no. 71, August 1977.
10. *200 Years of the Trent & Mersey Canal*, bicentenary commemorative brochure, produced by the Trent & Mersey Canal Society, 1977.

# Index

References to illustrations are printed in *italics*

Abbey Wood, 60
Adams, William, 13, 55
Agde, 17
Agden, 20, 26
Aiken, John, 18
Aire & Calder Canal, 67, 90
Aldersley, 147
Allport, J., 140
Alrewas, 38, *111, 119,* 127
Alton, 56, 60, 63
Alton Wire Mill, 60, 62
Anderton, 30, 86-8, 98, 129-30, 135
    *136,* 137-8, 144, 146, 155
Anderton Co, carriers, 98, 122, 137
    145, 149
Anderton Lift, *66,* 137-8, *139,* 140,
    162
Anker River, 76
Anson, Lord, 15
Apedale, 81
Apedale Collieries, 78, 131
Arkwright, Richard, 14
Armitage tunnel, 36, 47, 158
Arrol, Sir William, & Co, 152
Ashbourne, 63
Ashby Canal, 81
Ashton Canal, 67
Astbury, John, 13, 27
Athelstone, 76
Atherstone, 39, 76-7
Autherley, 70

Bagnall, John, 55

Bagnall reservoir, 59
Bagot, Sir Walter, 26
Banbury, 35
Banks, Sir Joseph, 36, 46
Barlaston, 161-2
Barnton tunnel, 36, 46, 86-7, 145
Barton Boat Co, 103
Bass, Michael, 73
Batchacre, 24
Bateman, T., 31
Bath Pool Valley, 106
Bedworth, 75
Bedworth Colliery, 75
Beech, John, 56
Beech & Co, 58
Benbow, C., 159
Bennett, Abraham, 14
Bennett, Arnold, 14
Bennett, C.E., 42
Bennett, John, 14
Bennett, Mary, 14
Bentley, Thomas, 18-20, 22-4, 26-8,
    33
Biddulph, 17
Bignall End, 81
Bill, Charles, 54
Bill, Robert, 56
Birchenwood Gas & Coke Co, 153
Birmingham, 19-20, 23-4, 28, 31,
    49, 51, 70-1, 73, 77, 80, 95-6,
    112-14, 121, 133, 142, 147
Birmingham & Derby Junction
    Railway, 116

Birmingham & Fazeley Canal, 75-7
Birmingham & Liverpool Junction
  Canal, 68, 70, 112-13, 135
Birmingham & Liverpool Ship Canal
  project, 142-3
Birmingham & London Junction
  Canal project, 112
Birmingham Canal, 75-6
Bond End Canal, 72-3, 141
Boothen, 12
Bosley, 68
Boston, 99
Botteslow, 12
Boughey, George, 80
Boulton, Matthew, 19
Bowes Committee of Inquiry into
  Inland Waterways (1958), 153
Bradford, Henry, 18
Bradwell, 13
Bramah, Joseph, 129
Brassington, John, 103
Braunston, 82, 112
Breedon limestone works, 46
Brentford, 82
Brick House Works, 13
Briddon's cotton works, 63
Bridgewater, Francis Egerton, 3rd
  Duke of, 11-12, 14-15, 17, 20, 22,
  24-6, 29-31, 35-6, 40, 42-3, 45,
  68, 86, 88-92
Bridgewater Canal, 17, 20, 23, 25,
  28-9, 31, 36, 40, 42, 44, *65*, 67,
  97, 99, 103, 113, 118, 122, 124,
  128, 130, 138, 146
Bridgewater Trustees, 115, 121
  123-5, 128, 135, 137, 145
Brindley, Anne, 44
Brindley, James, 14-18, 23, 26-7,
  30-1, 33, 35-7, 39, 42-4, 48, 57,
  103, 160, 162
Brindley, John, 14
Brindley, Matthew, 62
Bristol, 24, 26, 103, 125
British Gas Light Co, 127
British Transport Commission, 150,
  155
British Transport Commission
  Yacht Club, 154

British Transport Waterways, 151,
  154, 159
British Waterways Board, 154-6,
  158, 160, 162
Brittain's Paper Mills, 150
Broade, Thomas, 15
Broken Cross, 87
Bromley Common, 41, 49
Brook, Sir Richard, 31, 40
Brown, Capability, 99
Brownhills, 31
Brunner Mond works, 141, 146, 148
Buckingham, Marquis of, 103
Buckley, J., 129
Bucknall, 55, 74
Bugsworth, 67
Burslem, 12-16, 19, 23-4, 26-7, 31-2,
  36, 51, 71, 74, 104, 123-4, 127-9,
  137, 151, 154-5
Burslem branch, 71-2
Burton Boat Co, 72
Burton-on-Trent, 11, 16-17, 40, 46,
  51, 63, 72-3, 81-2, 86, 100, *111*,
  116, 141-2, 146-7, 156, 162
Buxton, 35
Byerley, Thomas, 91-2
Byng, Hon John, 99, 104

Caernarvonshire Militia, 52
Caister, 89
Calder & Hebble Navigation, 67
Caldon branch, 54-5, 57-60, 63-4,
  67-8, *79*, 81, *84*, 95-6, *101*, 114,
  150, 155, 157, 161
Caldon Canal Society, 157-8
Caldon lime works, 54-7, 59-60, 141,
  148
Caldon Low, 54, 56, 58, 60, 141, 148
Caldwell, James, 69-70, 106, 108,
  110
California lock, 63
Castle Donington, 99
Castlefield, 17
Castle Northwich, 87
Cavendish Bridge, 73, 99
Cavendish Bridge Boat Co, 88
Cerebos Ltd, 155
Cheadle, 56, 60, 63, 81

Cheadle Brass Co, 60, 62
Checkley Brook, 24, 26
Cheddleton, 55, 57, 64, 150, 158
Cheshire, 11, 13, 18, 22, 24, 27-9,
  31, 45, 64, 70, 78, 80, 86, 89, 92,
  97-8, 114, 123, 151, 154, 156
Chester, 23, 35, 42, 49, 63, 110, 115
Chester Canal, 35, 63-4, 70, 82
Churchill, Winston, 148
Churnet, River, 56-7, 62-3, 107,
  116, 158
Churnet Valley Railway, 117
Civic Trust, 162
Clay Cross Co, 148
Clayton, 12
Coalbrookdale, 71
Coalport, 71
Cobridge, 71
Cockshute siding, 155
Coleshill, 75-6
Collins, Christina, 160
Colwich, *102*, 116
Commercial Canal project, 81-2
Congleton, 28
Congreve, Thomas, 17
Consall, 55, 57-8, 158
Copestake, Henry, 56
Corbyn's Hall, 124
Cornwall, 114-15, 140, 146
Cornwallis, Earl of, 112
Cotton Common, 58
Coventry, 35, 39, 75, 77
Coventry Canal, 35, 39, 44, 75-7,
  81-2, 92, 125, 146-7
*Cranford*, 45
Craven, Earl of, 112
Crewe, 130, 133
Cromford, 68
Cromford Canal, 122
Cromford & High Peak Railway, 68,
  112, 122
Crosley, William, 68
Crown Inn, Shardlow, 100
Crown Inn, Stone, 33
Croxton, 144
Crump Wood, 63

Dadford, Thomas, 76

Dale Hall, 71
Dallow Lane, 156
Dane, River, 27, 30, 107-8
Darwin, Erasmus, 12, 18-19, 23-4
Davies, D. P., 48
Dee, River, 35, 110
Delft, 13
Denby, 78
Denford, 67, *101*
Denstone, 117
Derby, 49, 78, 99
Derby Canal, 78, 146, 161
Derbyshire, 11, 14-15, 19, 27, 29,
  31, 48, 99, 148
Derbyshire County Council, 161
Derwent River, 98
Derwent Mouth, 41, 49, 78, 127,
  146, 156
Devon, 13, 114
Devonshire, Duke of, 67
Dew, George, & Co., 153
Dilhorne, 81
Disley, 67
Donnington Wood Canal, 22, 71
Dorset, 114, 146
Doulton Co, 129
Dove, River, 45
Doveholes, 67
Dukinfield Junction, 67
Dundee Chamber of Commerce, 148
Dunlop Rubber Co, 161
Dyke, Benjamin, 97

Eaves in Whiston, 54
Edgeworth, R. L., 51
Egerton, Francis, *see* Bridgewater,
  Duke of
Egerton, Samuel, 28, 30, 45, 51, 58
Egginton, 45
Elers, David and John, 13
Ellesmere & Chester Canal, 70-1,
  112, 115, 135
Ellesmere Port, 115, 137
Endon, 57, 63-4, 67
Erewash Canal, 78
Etruria, 19, 32-3, 43, 49, 52, 57,
  71, 85, 90, 96-7, 100, *102*, 104-
  105, 123-4, 128, 137, 155, 161

Etruria Hall, 32, 43, 91, 104-5, 161
Exeter Canal, 17
Eyes, surveyor, 18

Faram, William, 69
Farey, John, 57-9
Farley, 54
Fazeley, 16, 39, 75-7
Federation of British Industries, 148
Fellows, Morton & Clayton Co, carriers, 145, 147, 149
Fenton, 12
Fenton, Vivian, 12
Flack, William, carrier, 99
Flaxman, John, 13, 92
Fleetstones, 72
Flint Mill lock, 114
Ford Green ironworks, 58
Fosbrooke, Leonard, 100
Fowlea Brook, 32
Foxley branch canal, 58, 150
Fradley, 39, 72, 75-7, 82, 85, 96, 116, *119*, 127-8, 146-7, 154
Froghall, 43, 46, 54-6, 58-60, 62-3, 67, 82, 117, 146, 148, 155, 158

Gainsborough, 16, 41, 44, 49, 73, 96, 99-100, 103, 121
Garbett, Samuel, 20, 22-3, 30
Garston, 58
Garston-Foxt lane, 58
Gaskell, Elizabeth, 45, 92
Geddes, Sir Eric, 148-9
George, David Lloyd, 148
Gilbert, John, 14, 17, 22-3, 30, 40, 54, 56, 88, 92, 103
Gilbert, Thomas, 14, 20, 22, 26-7, 56-7, 92
Golborne, John, 20, 28
Golden Hill, 44
Golden Hill Colliery, 14
Gower, Earl, Granville, *see* Stafford, Marquess of
Grand Junction Canal, 64, 73, 82, 112, 125
Grand Junction Railway, 113-14, 116-17, 121, 130
Grantham, 99

Gravesend, 114
Great Haywood, 17, 41, 57, *93*, 100, 121, 123, 127, 146
Great Western Railway, 146, 149
Gresley, Nigel Bowyer, 78, 80
Gresley, Sir Nigel, 78, 80-1
Grey, Lord, 26

Hadfield, Charles, 41, 75, 81
Hall Green branch, 68-9, 70, 127, 133, 146
Hamilton, George E., 110
Hanley, 12-13, 23, 55, 71, *84*, 104, 129, 157
Hardings Wood, 68-9, 85, 104
Harecastle tunnel, 14, 16, 24, 26, 33, 36-9, 44-5, 47, 51, 54-5, 68-69, 82, *83*, 96, 103, 105-10, 112, 127, 142-5, 153, 158-61
Hardman, John, 18
Hawkesbury, 76
Hayes Colliery, 123
Hayne, George, 100
Haywood, *see* Great Haywood
Hazelhurst, 64
Hazelhurst aqueduct, 67, *101*
Hazelhurst locks, 64, *84*
Harston Wood, 58
Heathcote, Robert E., 131
Hemingslow Quarry, 58
Hempstones, 20, 29
Henshall, Hugh, 14-16, 31, 33, 41, 44, 46-8, 55, 96, 104
Henshall, Hugh & Co, carriers, 49, 88-9, 91, 96, 117
Heron, George, 24
Hertford, Marquis of, 112
Hill, Richard, 54, 56
Hill, Sir Rowland, 31
Hock Hill, 39
Hollinhurst, 67
Holly Bush Inn, *101*
Horncastle, 99
Horninglow, 81, 100, 116, 162
Huddlesford, 39
Huish, Captain Mark, 130
Hull, 11, 23-7, 51, 73, 75, 82, 99-100, 103, 121, 145-6

Humber, River, 147

ICI, 141, 154
Inland Waterways Redevelopment
  Committee, 154, 157
Ipstones, 43
Ivy House Works, 13

Jackson's Wood, 63
Jessop, Josiah, 68
Jessop, William, 68, 81, 90
Johnson Brothers, 157

Kenwright, William, 100
Ketley, 71
Kidsgrove, *50*
Kidsgrove Boggart, 160
King's Bromley Common, 15-16
Kingsley, 56
Kingsley Moor Collieries, 60
Kingswinford, 124
Knutsford, 26, 28, 45, 67
Knutton Junction, 131
Knypersley reservoir, 59, 107-8,
  110, 112

Lambeth, 129
Lancashire, 27-9, 125
Lane Delph, 71
Lane End, 12, 71, 74
Langley Mill, 78
Languedoc, Grand Canal of, 17
*Lapwing,* 160
Lawton, 27, 36, 51, 68-9, 80, 104
Lawton, John, 29
Lead, Peter, 57, 81
Leeds & Liverpool Canal, 44
Leek, 14, 43, 45-6, 63-4, 68, 148,
  150
Leek branch, 64, 82, 150, 158
Leek Urban District Council, 158
Lehane, Mackenzie & Shand, 159
Leicester, 49, 99
Leicestershire, 27
Leicestershire & Northamptonshire
  Union Canal, 125
Leigh, Edward, 56
Lichfield, 15-16, 19-20, 27, 45, 49,
  51-2, 95

Lilleshall, 71
Lincoln, 99, 121
Lincolnshire, 27, 122
Little Eaton, 63, 78
Liverpool, 11, 18, 20, 22-8, 35, 40,
  42-3, 49-50, 70-1, 73, 75, 82,
  86-7, 89-91, 96-7, 99, 103, 112-
  114, 121-4, 133, 135, 146, 160
Liverpool & Manchester Railway,
  113
Liverpool Corporation, 18
Lloyd, Sampson, 39
Loch, George, 121-2
Loch, James, 115, 121
Loch, Joseph, 113
London, 19, 27-8, 44, 51, 70, 73,
  80-2, 95, 103, 112-14, 122, 127,
  160
London & North Western Railway,
  113, 121, 124-5, 130, 133, 135,
  140
London & Birmingham Railway,
  117, 121
London & North Eastern Railway,
  149
London, Midland & Scottish Rail-
  way, 148-50
Longbridge, 15-16
Longford, 20, 39, 75-6
Longport, 71, 87, 90, 96, 100, 103,
  123-4, 137, 155
Longton, 12, 71, 114
Loughborough, 99
Lunar Society, 19

Macclesfield, 14, 24, 26, 28-9, 64,
  67-8, 116, 133
Macclesfield Canal, 29, 67-70, 112,
  118, 128, 132, 146
Macclesfield Copper Co, 29
Madeley, 130, 132
Malet, Hugh, 17, 40
Malt Shovel Inn, 100, *120*
Manchester, 11, 17, 23-5, 28, 40,
  49, 52, 67, 70-1, 73, 82, 88-9,
  91-2, 97, 99, 103, 110, 112, 114,
  121-2, 124, 133, 155

Manchester & Birmingham railway, 116, 121
Manchester & Leeds Railway, 122
Manchester & Salford Junction Canal, 128
Manchester Ship Canal, 141, 144
Mantoux, Paul, 14
Marbury, 128, 151
Marchay Colliery, 128
Market Drayton, 71, 131-2, 151
Market Harborough, 99
Marlborough, 54
Marple, 64, 67-8
Marston, 151, 153
Matthews, William, 124-5
Meaford, 105
Mellor, 67
Melton Mowbray, 99
Mersey, River, 11, 18, 20, 25-31, 42-3, 81, 86, 89, 135, 137, 144, 146-7, 151, 153-4, 156
Mersey & Irwell Canal, 25, 128
Mersey Weaver & Ship Canal Carrying CO, 98, 154
Middleport, 122
Middlewich, 28, 30, 35, 43, 46, *50*, 51, 70, 85, 87-9, 144, 146, 155-156, 162
Middlewich branch, 112, 115
Midland Railway, 117, 140, 145
Milton, 55, 150, 157
*Milton Maid*, 157
*Milton Queen*, 157
Ministry of Transport, 149, 155, 157
Ministry of War Transport, 150
Ministry of Ways and Communications, 148
Minton, Thomas, 13
Mitchell, Charles, 124
Moira, Earl of, 73
Morris, P., 133
Morris's lock, *see* California lock
Mowlen Northern Ltd, 159
Mytton, Thomas, 56

Nailor, T., 31
Nantwich, 35, 64, 70, 81

National Coal Board, 151, 153
Navigation Inn, 100
Nether Knutsford, 24
Newcastle, manor of, 12
Newcastle, Thomas, Duke of, 73
Newcastle-under-Lyme, 12, 15-16, 19-20, 25, 27, 52, 78, 80-1, 131-2
Newcastle-under-Lyme Canal, 78, 80-1, 131
Newcastle-under-Lyme Canal Extension Railway, 131
Newcastle-under-Lyme Junction Canal, 80-1, 131
Newark, 49, 90, 99, 121
Newchapel, 44
Newdigate, Sir Roger, 44
Newhaven, 114
Norbury Colliery, 68
North Rode, 116
North Staffordshire Chamber of Commerce, 144
North Staffordshire Railway, 116-118, 121-5, 128, 130-3, 135, 137-8, 140-8
Northwich, 12, 20, 22, 26, *34*, 86-88, 98, 128, 141, 151, 162
Norton, 55, 58, 158
Norton, Peter, 145
Norton Biddulph, 74
Norton Bridge, 116, 133
Norton Green Colliery, 58, 158
Norton Hall, 31, 40
Norton Priory, 40
Nottingham, 17, 23, 49, 78, 99-100, 147
Nottinghamshire, 27, 122
Nuneaton, 39
Nuttall, John, 67

Oakamoor, 60, 62, 117
Oakmeadow Ford, 57, 114
Oldham, 153
Oldham, Hugh, 28
Oldknow, Samuel, 67
Outram, Benjamin, 64, 68, 78
Oxford, 39, 75, 77
Oxford Canal, 39, 44, 75-6, 81-2

Paget, William, Lord, *see* Uxbridge, Earl of
Parrott, R., 31
Partridge Nest, 81
Pave Lane, 71
Peak Forest Canal, 64, 67-8, 122, 132
Penk, River, 17
Penkhull, 12
Pennant, Thomas, 51-2
Peover Eye Brook, 30
Peover, River, 27
Phillips, John, 24, 38
Phillipps, W. Douglas, 143, 145-6
Pickford & Co, 97, 122, 160
Pool Dam, 131
Potter, James, 69, 106, 108-10
Potteries, 12-14, 20, 24, 29, 32, 44, 51, 71, 74, 78, 81-2, 86, 90-1, 97, 100, 104, 113-14, 116-17, 121, 123, 129-33, 135, 137, 140, 142, 146-7, 153-6, 161
Potteries Chamber of Commerce, 128, 137, 140
Potteries Wakes, 154
Poynton Colliery, 68
Preston Brook, 12, 29, 31, *34*, 40, 43, 46, 49, 51, *65*, 86, 89-91, 103, 116, 121-4, 127-30, 132-3, 135, 137, 142, 146, 156, 160
Preston Brook tunnel, 36, 39, 43-4, *65*, 127, 145
Preston Hill, 39
Price, Sir Frank, 160
Priestley, Joseph, 19
*Prince Regent*, 63
Pritchard, D., & Hoof, W., canal contractors, 69, 109
Pybus, John, 95

Quinton's Wood, 80

Railway & Canal Traffic Act (1888), 134, 143
Railway Executive Committee, 148, 158
Rangeley & Dixon, 105
Reading, 44

Reid, Alexander, & Co, carriers, 98
Rennie, John, 37, 60, 105-7
Ricardo, John Lewis, 117-18
Rickman, 109
Ridge House estate, 32
Rocester, 63, 117
Rock Services (Midlands) Ltd, 158
Rochdale Canal, 67
Rode Hall, 36
Rode Heath, 151
Roe, Charles, 24
Royal Commission on Canals and Waterways (1906-9), 145
Rudyard reservoir, 63-4, 106, 108, 144, 154, 158
Rugeley, 27, 45, *93*, 156
Runcorn, 25, 29-30, 35, 40, 42-3, 103, 113, 124, 130, 132, 140, 142, 146
Runcorn & Weston Canal, 128
Rusholme, Lord, 153
Rushton Grange, Vill of, 12

St John's Square, 72
St Petersburg, 73
Saltersford tunnel, 36, 46, 145
Sale Moor, 28
Salt Union, carriers, 146, 154
Sandbach, 46,123, 146, 148
Sandiacre, 78
Sandon, 57
Sankey Brook (St Helens) Canal, 17, 22
Scropton, 19
Seabridge, 12
Seddon, Henry, 155
Selby, 122
Severn River, 11, 17-18, 24, 75, 123
Shakespeare Inn, 100
Shand (Midlands), 159
Shardlow, 49, 78, 86, 88, 97-100, 103, 116, *120*, *122*, *126*, 127, 142, 161
Shardlow Hall, 99-100
Sheasby, Thomas, 76
Sheffield, Ashton & Manchester Railway, 132

Shelton, 12, 32, 56-7, 71, 74, 103, 127, 161
Shelton ironworks, 43, 128
Shirley Hollow, 58
Shirley Common, 58
Shobnall, 72-3, 116
Shrewsbury, 71
Shrewsbury, Earl of, 54, 56, 60, 62
Shropshire Union Main Line, 112, 146, 156
Shropshire Union Railways & Canal Co, 135
Shugborough, 41
Sideway House, 71, 155
Silverdale, 131-2
Silverdale & Newcastle-under-Lyme Railway, 131
Silverdale ironworks, 131
Simpson, Charles, 95
Simpson, Phoebe, 95
Sir Nigel Gresley's Canal, 78, 80-81, 131
Slain Hollow, 60
Sleaford, 99
Smeaton, John, 15-16
Smiles, Samuel, 14, 32
Smith, Fereday, 115
Smith, George, 54, 56
South Derbyshire District Council, 161
Sneyd, 12
Sneyd, Edward, 45, 48, 58
Sneyd, John, 45
Sneyd, Ralph, 131
Soresby, John, 99, 122
South Western Co, 146
Southern Fleet, 155
Southern Railway, 149
Sparrow, John, 25, 27-8, 31, 33, 39-40, 45, 54-5, 57, 78
Sparrow, Thomas, 72-4, 76-7
Spath, 62
Spode, Josiah, 13
Stafford, 24, 53, 60, 142
Stafford, John, 26-7
Stafford, Marquess of, 2nd Earl Gower, 14-15, 20, 22, 26, 30, 36, 90, 104, 127

Staffordshire, *passim*
Staffordshire & Worcestershire Canal, 17, 41, 70, 75, 121, 125, 146
Staffordshire County Council, 157-158
Stamford, Lord, 46
Stanley, 150
Stanley reservoir, 58-9, 154
Star Inn, 105
Stephenson, George, 131
Stevens & Co, 99
Stevenson, Elizabeth, *see* Gaskell, Elizabeth
Stockport, 24, 28, 67
Stockton locks, 64
Stockton Quay, 103, 124
Stoke-on-Trent, 12, 14-15, 19, 23, 44-5, 57, *61*, 71, 80-1, 85, 90-91, 100, 103-4, 124, 129-31, 137, 142, 155-6, 162
Stoke-on-Trent Boat Club, 158
Stoke-on-Trent City Council, 157-8
Stoke 'D' Road, 162
Stone, 27, 33, 35, 41, 44, 57, *61*, 62, 71, 74, 85, 105, 108, 110, 112, 116, 122, 162
Stourport, 17, 49, 88-9, 96, 103
Stour, River, 17
Stratford-on-Avon Canal, 112
Stubbs Walk, 80-1, 131
Stub Wood, 62
Sutton, James, 98-9, 117, 122, 127
Sutton, Robinson & Co, carriers, 97
Swan Inn, *119*
Swan Line cruisers, 154
Swarkestone, 27, 39, 78, 116, *126*, 127, 146, 161
Swarkestone Boat Club, 161

Talke, 81
Tame, River, 16, 18, 76-7
Tamworth, 15-16, 18-19
Tatton Park, 45
Taylor, surveyor, 18
Tean, River, 63
Teesside, 154

Telford, Thomas, 68-9, 107-10, 112, 160
*Tench*, 156
Thurlwood, 151-3
Tittensor, 81
Toulouse, 17
Traders (North Staffordshire) Carrying Co Ltd, 137
Transport Act (1947), 150
Transport Act (1962), 155
Transport Act (1968), 156, 158
Trent & Mersey Canal Society, 161-162
Trent Canal project, 77-8
Trentham, 22, 42, 57, 155-6
Trent, River, 11, 13, 15-19, 24, 26-27, 29-30, 38, 40-1, 44-5, 72-3, 78, 80-1, 98-100, 116, 122, 127, 141-2, 145-6
Trent Vale, 132
Trent Valley Railway, 116, 121
Trubshaw, James, 110
Trubshaw Colliery, 127
Tunstall, 12, 103, 135
Tunsted, 14
Turnhurst, 14-15, 44
Twyford, Thomas, 129

Ubberley, 74
Upper Cotton, 60, 141
Uttoxeter, 13, 60, 62-3, 81-2, 116-117
Uttoxeter branch, 60, 62-3, 82, 117
Uxbridge, Earl of, 40, 72-3, 80, 100

Vale Pleasant, 71
Vaughan, William, 112

Wade Brook, 30
Ward, J. R., 95
Wardle, 70, 128, 133, 146
Wardle Green branch, 70-1, 114-116
Warrington, 22, 103, 124, 127
Warrington Academy, 19
Waterhouses, 148
*Water Lapwing*, 154-5

Warwick, 92
Warwickshire, 27
Warwickshire Militia, 103
Waterworks lock, 158
Watt, James, 19
Weaver, River, 12, 13, 16, 18-20, 22, 24, 26-7, 29-30, 43, 46-7, *66*, 85-8, 98, 130-1, 137-8, 142, 146
Weaver, trustees, 11-12, 20, 22, 24-25, 29, 43, 85, 98, 129, 132, 135, 137-8
Wedgwood, Francis, 105
Wedgwood, Godfrey, 137
Wedgwood, Henry, 105
Wedgwood, John, 14, 15, 23, 25-6, 91
Wedgwood, Josiah, 12-13, 18-20, 22-7, 30-3, 35, 39, 41, 43-6, 51, 53-4, 59, 75, 78, 82, 85-92, 95-6, *102*, 104, 162
Wedgwood, Ken, 153
Wedgwood Sons & Byerley, 91
Wedgwood, Thomas, junior, 19
Wedgwood, Thomas, senior, 14, 19
Wellington, 131
Wesley, John, 51
Weston-on-Trent, 41, 49, 98
Weston Point Docks, 130, 137, 155
Whaley Bridge, 67-8
Wheelock River, 151
Whieldon, Sampson, 54, 56
Whieldon's Grove, 114
Whiston, 58, 60
Whitfield coal-mines, 59
Whitmore, 130
Whittington Brook, 75-6, 94
Whitworth, Robert, 76, 81
Whitworth, Sir Richard, 24, 26, 30-1
Wilbraham, Sir Randle, 36
Wilden Ferry, 15-18, 20, 23, 25-8, 30, 33, 38-40, 44-5, 51, 72, 99-100
Willan, T. S., 30
Williams, E. Leader, 138
Willington, 27, 128
Wilne Ferry, *see* Wilden Ferry
Wilson, Robert J., 122

Wincham, 85, 130
Wincham Brook, 30
Wincham Mill, 30
Winsford, 20, 22, 24, 26, 48, 86-7,
    98, 142
Witton Bridge, 24, 28, 30, 67
Witton Common, 30
Wollaton, 100
Wolseley Bridge, 26-7, 38
Wolseley, Sir William, 26
Wolstanton, 12
Wolverhampton, 28, 49, 121-2,
    142, 147
Woodhead Hall, 63
Woodhead Plateway, 63
Woodstanton, 48
Wooliscroft, William, 56

Worcester & Birmingham Canal,
    121
Worcestershire, 154
Wormhill, 14
Worsley, 11, 17, 36, 54, 59
Worthington & Gilbert, canal
    carriers, 88-9
Worthington, William & Sons, 73
Wright, Samuel, 26
Wrinehill, 24
Wrottesley, Sir John, 39
Wychnor, 20, 27, 38, 73
Wychnor Church, 38, *120*

Yardley, Benjamin, 55
Yorkshire, 13, 27
Young, Arthur, 38